LAURA CANDLER'S

POWER READING WORKSHOP

LAURA CANDLER'S
POWER READING WORKSHOP
A STEP-BY-STEP GUIDE

COMPASS

A DIVISION OF BRIGANTINE MEDIA

For more information about site licenses or multiple copies, visit the resource page
online for this book:
www.lauracandler.com/prw
or
Brigantine Media
211 North Avenue
Saint Johnsbury, Vermont 05819
Phone: 802-751-8802
E-mail: neil@brigantinemedia.com
Website: www.brigantinemedia.com

Acknowledgments

Writing *Laura Candler's Power Reading Workshop* has truly been an act of collaboration. I couldn't have written this book without the help and inspiration of the teachers below and many others who did not choose to be acknowledged. I knew that the reading workshop approach worked in my own classroom, but I wanted to create a guide that would work in virtually any upper elementary classroom. The strategies I shared during the development of this book were tested and adapted by hundreds of teachers, and they were tweaked to make them work in classrooms all over the world. I received many excellent suggestions to improve the content and wording of the original manuscript. I feel blessed to have had the opportunity to work with these teachers. I know that if I were to walk into any of their classrooms, I would find kids who love to read and who are empowered by that love.

—*Laura Candler*

● ● ● ● ● ● ● ● ●

Kristin Smith
Angola, IN

Beth Shmagin
Los Angeles, CA

Mary Chriss
Carmel, IN

Mariah Monroe
Occidental, CA

Anne McCarthy
Oviedo, FL

Erin Duarte
Sacramento, CA

Sarah Biron
Quinebaug, CT

Claire Torrey
Chanhassen, MN

Jenny Owens
Cumming, GA

Linda Schuman
West Palm Beach, FL

Judith Rowe
Australia

Vallerie Sharp
Hagerstown, IN

Loren Van De Griek
Hickory, NC

Diane Harrison
Toccoa, GA

Melissa Cowden
Bloomington, IN

Francie Kugelman
Los Angeles, CA

Joelle Eiden
Holly Springs, NC

Rebecca Barta
Killeen, TX

Theresa Adams
Hamilton, Ontario

Lisa Vail
Wilmington, NC

Tammi Purdin
North Port, FL

Debby Hickey
Goldsboro, NC

Krystal Van Kampen
Jacksonville, FL

Jewelia Oswald
Topeka, KS

Melissa Zipperian
Gillette, WY

Stacy Hersey
Goldsboro, NC

Barb Decker
Momence, IL

Ann Corto Goldbach
Liberty Township, Ohio

Julia Neilson
Tasmania, Australia

Terri Bunch
Atlanta, GA

Pamela Moll
Oviedo, FL

Dena Oneal
Murfreesboro, TN

Heather Richards
Odessa, TX

Christine Dewees
Jacksonville, FL

Linda Bruno
Bristol, RI

Julie Marcus
Spring Lake, MI

Tara Bishop
Albuquerque, NM

Meg Basker
Mishawaka, IN

Jeremy Aten
Taylorsville, NC

Nancy Foote
Gilbert, AZ

Kristin Kuntz
Winchester, VA

Sandy Brown
Scottsdale, AZ

Merideth Fisher
McLean, VA

Shelley Houle
Camas, WA

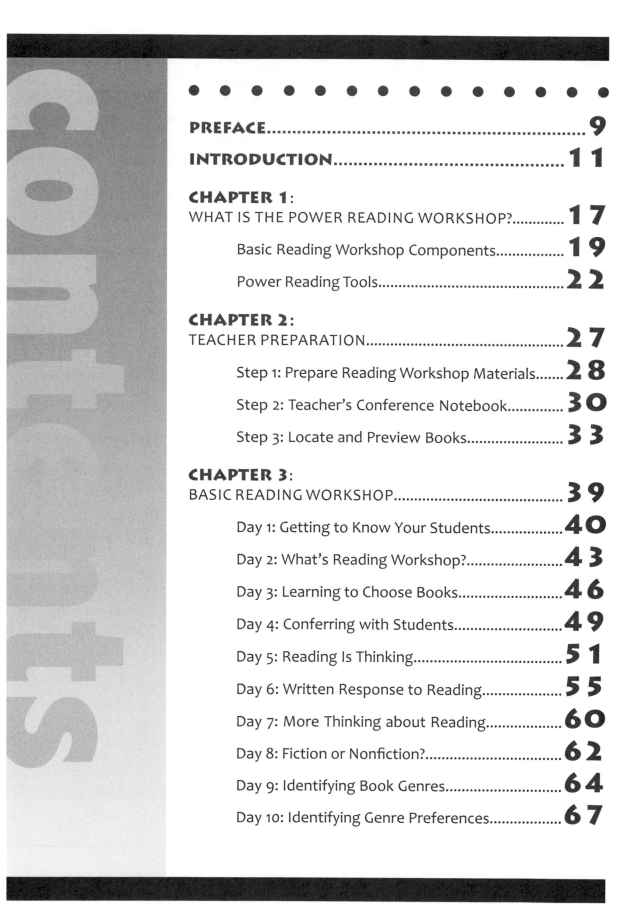

PREFACE..**9**

INTRODUCTION..................................**11**

CHAPTER 1:
WHAT IS THE POWER READING WORKSHOP?............**17**

    Basic Reading Workshop Components................**19**

    Power Reading Tools...**22**

CHAPTER 2:
TEACHER PREPARATION...**27**

    Step 1: Prepare Reading Workshop Materials.......**28**

    Step 2: Teacher's Conference Notebook..............**30**

    Step 3: Locate and Preview Books......................**33**

CHAPTER 3:
BASIC READING WORKSHOP.......................................**39**

    Day 1: Getting to Know Your Students................**40**

    Day 2: What's Reading Workshop?.....................**43**

    Day 3: Learning to Choose Books......................**46**

    Day 4: Conferring with Students........................**49**

    Day 5: Reading Is Thinking...............................**51**

    Day 6: Written Response to Reading..................**55**

    Day 7: More Thinking about Reading.................**60**

    Day 8: Fiction or Nonfiction?............................**62**

    Day 9: Identifying Book Genres.........................**64**

    Day 10: Identifying Genre Preferences................**67**

CHAPTER 4:
POWER READING TOOLS.. **73**

Tool 1: Power Reading Logs................................. **77**

Tool 2: Everyday Reading: Fiction or Nonfiction?... **78**

Tool 3: Flexible Guided Reading Groups............. **81**

Tool 4: Book Challenges..................................... **84**

Tool 5: Personal Goal Setting............................. **93**

Tool 6: Extended Written Response................... **96**

Tool 7: Audio Books.. **102**

Tool 8: Book Buzz.. **105**

Tool 9: Magazine Power Hour....................... **109**

Tool 10: Graphic Organizers......................... **113**

Tool 11: Self Assessment.............................. **120**

Tool 12: Strategic Planning.......................... **124**

APPENDIX:
ADDITIONAL RESOURCES........................... **129**

Activities and Interests.................................. **130**

Book Challenge Certificates.......................... **132**

Professional Reading..................................... **135**

Internet Resources.. **136**

Books for the First Ten Days......................... **137**

Books for Older Readers............................... **139**

Notes.. **141**

PREFACE

• • • • • • • • •

The book you're holding is the tangible result of a dream I have treasured for almost thirty years.

I have always loved to read, but when I began teaching, it was disturbing to discover that most of my students didn't share this passion. Why couldn't they see that reading a book was like watching an amazing movie in your mind—a private movie created from the author's words and the reader's imagination? I was determined to change their perceptions about reading.

For the next two decades, I tried everything, from SSR to basal reading programs to literacy centers, in an effort to turn reluctant readers into lifelong readers. The result? I discovered that while I could bribe them to read and coax higher reading scores from them, I couldn't seem to inspire them to love reading the way I do.

Then a few years ago I discovered an entirely new way to teach reading—the Reading Workshop method, where students read their own books and have individual conferences with the teacher. This approach intrigued me with its simplicity, but I wondered if it could work in today's climate of testing and teacher accountability.

I began to research the method in more detail, and eventually I took a huge leap of faith and gave Reading Workshop a try. I began by implementing a basic Reading Workshop, and then I added a number of challenging strategies designed to produce measurable growth in reading skills. I modified some strategies and created a few of my own, carefully recording every step of the process. After just a few weeks, I began seeing results, and I realized that I was on to something. I had found a way to teach reading that not only improved skills but inspired kids to love books!

After a few months, I began sharing the strategies with other teachers. I wanted to know if these methods could be applied in other classrooms with the same degree of success. I created an e-mail discussion group, the Empowering Readers Learning Community, and I started writing the manuscript that would eventually become this step-by-step guide to Reading Workshop. The original version of this book was titled *Empowering Readers: A Quick-Start Guide to Reading Workshop,* and it was only available in digital form. As members of the discussion group began to implement the strategies, they offered feedback and helped me tweak the methods to make them even more effective.

Soon, teachers were sharing their success stories with the discussion group, and my faith in Reading Workshop was affirmed on every level. Not only were their students begging for more time to read, they were becoming better readers in measurable ways!

The early success of the digital book motivated me to seek a publisher for a print version. A series of fortunate events led me to Neil Raphel and Janis Raye of Brigantine Media, who immediately recognized the uniqueness of this book as well as its potential. Together we reorganized and reformatted the content of the book, creating an even more powerful resource for teachers. They proposed a new title, *Laura Candler's Power Reading Workshop: A Step-by-Step Guide,* which more effectively describes my program. The makeover became complete with a brand-new cover and more professional photographs to accompany the written strategies.

In print form, the book will be widely available to educators who seek a better way to teach reading, a method that not only results in better readers, but also inspires kids to love reading. Yet as I reflect on the new title, I must point out that while I did develop the specific step-by-step method you'll find in *Power Reading Workshop,* the entire model was actually the result of collaboration among many fine educators. That's why we call it "Field Tested/Teacher Approved."

I invite you to adapt the strategies and make them your own. In fact, I have absolute faith in your ability to use these methods to transform your classroom.

Think of these steps as a special recipe for Reading Workshop, but remember that any recipe can be improved by adding a dash of this and a sprinkle of that! Like a world-class chef, you'll experiment until you discover just the right ingredients to serve up success in your own classroom. And after your students taste the joys of reading, they'll develop a lifelong appetite for books!

●　●　●　●　●　●　●　●　●

INTRODUCTION

• • • • • • • • • •

Do your students love to read? If they're like many kids today, they spend far more time watching TV, texting their friends, and playing video games than they do reading. It's not that they can't read—they just choose not to do so. With today's accountability laws, we have done a commendable job of teaching reading skills. However, we've fallen far short of instilling a passion for reading.

What if you had the power to change your students' attitudes about reading? Believe it or not, the task isn't difficult, but it does require a willingness to abandon methods that aren't working in favor of more effective strategies. Thousands of teachers have experienced success using a simple yet powerful model called Reading Workshop. This method uses a combination of mini-lessons, independent reading time, and individual conferences to inspire and motivate students.

After researching this approach for several years, I began implementing the basic model that was described in many books and on numerous websites. However, I sensed that something more was needed to produce exceptional results. I loved the idea of students reading their own books, but I also wanted to be sure that they were continually challenged to improve as readers. To address these needs, I adapted a few strategies, and I created a number of my own techniques. I began referring to these extra components as my "Power Reading Tools" and the entire program as the "Power Reading Workshop."

Almost from the beginning, I began to see the impact of Reading Workshop on my students. Not only did they love to read, it was clear that they were becoming better readers as well. I knew I had to write a book to share these strategies with others. *Laura Candler's Power Reading Workshop: A Step-by-Step Guide* offers an easy, step-by-step plan for effective reading instruction. First, I'll show you how to set up a basic Reading Workshop in your own classroom. Then I'll describe how to turn the basic program into a Power Reading Workshop by adding strategies that motivate and challenge your students to take responsibility for their personal growth as readers. Along the way, I share the reproducible activity pages and resources I've developed to make the program easy as well as effective.

Are you ready to start your own Power Reading Workshop? With this step-by-step guide, you can jump in and get started right away, tweaking the program along the way to make it perfect for your own students. When you do, you'll be amazed at how quickly you can empower your students with a love of reading!

Comprehensive Manual or Step-by-Step Guide?

When I decided to write this book, I realized that the market is saturated with excellent comprehensive books on how to implement Reading Workshop, but nowhere did I find a simple step-by-step guide. Through conversations with other teachers, it became clear to me that a resource to guide teachers through their implementation of the Reading Workshop program was desperately needed. Use this guide to help you get started, and then explore the wealth of additional books and resources on this topic. You'll find a list of additional resources in the Appendix, and they are definitely worth the time you'll invest in reading them.

Assumptions

I'm going to make some assumptions before we begin. If these assumptions aren't true regarding your classroom or your school environment, you may need to make some modifications to your Reading Workshop program.

YOU AS A READER ● First and foremost, I'm going to assume that you enjoy reading for pleasure and want to share your love of reading with your students. If you don't love to read, please explore your own feelings about reading before you attempt to influence your students. Read children's literature and talk with other educators to discover what types of books they enjoy. Perhaps your own experiences in school caused you to dislike reading. Take heart—it's not too late to change! Think you can fool your students into believing that you like to read when you don't? Think again!

COMPUTERIZED TEST PROGRAMS ● For the purposes of this book, I'm assuming that you will not be using a computerized test program such as Accelerated Reader or Reading Counts. If you do use one of these programs, please allow students to read other books as well and offer a way for students to earn "points" for books that are not on the list. Don't emphasize the rewards and the points when you talk to your students about their books; instead, focus on their growth as readers and the variety of genres in their reading choices. Teach kids to find pleasure in reading rather than in achieving external rewards and recognition.

ACCESS TO READING MATERIAL ● For this method, your students will need regular access to a variety of books and other reading material. If you don't have a full classroom library, your students will need to be able to visit the school library as needed, starting on the first day you introduce Reading Workshop.

BASAL READING PROGRAMS ● It will be difficult to fully implement a Reading Workshop if you are required to teach from a basal reading text. If you are required to use a basal reader, you'll need to get permission to try this alternate approach to reading instruction. Ask your administrator to let you try this approach for one grading period. Offer to review the results together to determine the program's effectiveness.

CLASSROOM MANAGEMENT ● If your classroom lacks an effective management system, now is not the time to begin using Reading Workshop. First, enlist the help of a mentor to work out an effective management system. Before allowing students the freedom inherent in Reading Workshop, they must consistently demonstrate respect for you, their classmates, and their classroom. Two excellent books on this topic are *The First Days of School* by Dr. Harry Wong, and *Tools for Teaching* by Dr. Fred Jones.

COOPERATIVE LEARNING ● Many of the activities described in the mini-lessons require students to work in cooperative learning teams or pairs. I have found partners or teams of four to be the most effective arrangement. If you are new to cooperative learning, I suggest that you obtain training on these strategies. Check out Dr. Spencer Kagan's *Cooperative Learning*, a comprehensive manual of specific and very effective techniques.

GUIDED READING INSTRUCTION ● After you set up your basic Reading Workshop, you'll probably want to add small guided reading groups as needed. Because there is a wealth of information on this topic, *Laura Candler's Power Reading Workshop* does not provide detailed instructions for this component. If you need specific, step-by-step instruction in how to use guided reading groups, I recommend the book, *Guided Reading in Grades 3-6: Everything You Need to Make Small-Group Reading Instruction Work in Your Classroom*, by Mary Browning Schulman. The book definitely fulfills the promise of its title.

READING PROFICIENCY ● Because this book is designed for grades two through six, I'm going to assume that most of your students can read on a minimal level or better. The Reading Workshop approach seems to be most effective with students who have mastered basic phonics skills but who need work in the areas of vocabulary, fluency, and comprehension. If most of your students are non-readers, use more explicit methods of reading instruction before starting a Reading Workshop.

● ● ● ● ● ● ● ● ●

CHAPTER 1

What Is the Power Reading Workshop?

WHAT IS THE POWER READING WORKSHOP?

• • • • • • • • • •

If you're not familiar with the Reading Workshop approach, you may be wondering what it looks like. Step into my room for a "virtual visit" and take a look. You might see me reading aloud, or see my students scattered around the room deep into their own books. Whether they are under desks or snuggled up with a pillow in the corner of the room, they'll scarcely notice as you step into the room. You might see me conferring with a few students as they make predictions or describe connections they made with their books. Small groups of students might be discussing a book or working on a graphic organizer together.

You might think that reading instruction isn't taking place. But a closer look will reveal that students are becoming more proficient readers in measurable ways. More importantly, as these students experience the joys of reading, they are becoming lifelong readers.

Parts of the Power Reading Workshop

The heart of Reading Workshop involves students choosing their own books and reading at their own pace for extended periods of time. But in order to be most effective, the Power Reading Workshop includes reading instruction as well as time to confer with students.

Where do you start? How do you create a program that's just right for your students? Don't worry! Just follow this simple "equation":

Basic Reading Workshop

+ Power Reading Tools

POWER READING WORKSHOP

Basic Reading Workshop includes:	**Power Reading Tools include:**
● Whole Class Read Alouds	● Goal Setting
● Strategy Mini-lessons	● Assessment and Reflection
● Self-Selected Reading Time	● Guided Reading Groups
● Individual Reading Conferences	● Extended Literary Response
● Response to Reading	● Strategic Planning

The step-by-step methods described in this book will guide you through the first ten days of implementing the Basic Reading Workshop. Then you'll learn a variety of strategies to add more depth after the basic components are in place. As you implement each step, you will adapt the model to fit your own classroom, creating your own unique Power Reading Workshop.

Basic Reading Workshop Components

Whole Class Read Alouds

Do you read aloud to your students? If not, be prepared to discover the joy of reading aloud and sharing great books with your students. Students from kindergarten through high school treasure the moments when their teachers read aloud to them.

In the Reading Workshop program, sometimes you'll read a short book and finish it that day. Other times you'll select a longer book that may take weeks or even months to complete. The times you spend reading and sharing great books will be some of the most special times of your day.

Reading aloud is much more than a "story time" in a Reading Workshop classroom. You'll use this time to teach the strategies and skills needed for students to become better readers.

Mini-lessons on Reading Strategies or Skills

Short mini-lessons provide the instructional heart of the Reading Workshop. Each mini-lesson targets a specific instructional objective—for example, making predictions, analyzing character traits and motives, inferring word meaning from context clues, or rereading to clarify understanding. Often, mini-lessons are based on the book you are reading aloud, but sometimes you'll use a supplementary text such as a news article, poem, or biography as the focus of your mini-lesson.

You'll find a list of reading strategies and skills on page 126. This list is not organized in a sequential manner; use it as a checklist to keep track of the skills you are teaching throughout the year.

Many of the books in the Professional Reading section on page 135 offer ideas to help you develop great mini-lessons.

Self-Selected Independent Reading

Allowing students to choose their own books and giving them time to read independently are the most critical elements of the Reading Workshop. They distinguish the Reading Workshop from other instructional models such as basal reader programs, whole class novel studies, or literature circles.

Let's examine how each element works in the Reading Workshop:

BOOK CHOICE ● In a true Reading Workshop, students may choose from a wide variety of fiction, nonfiction, poetry, and even magazine or newspaper articles. Furthermore, they are not required to select Accelerated Reader books or read books from a given list. Yes, students are guided to choose appropriate books, but they are not restricted from entire genres or specific reading levels.

Don't confuse book choice or "self-selected reading" with the method known as "SSR" or "sustained silent reading." In that SSR model, students read for a long period of time, and the teacher is often encouraged to pick up a book and read during this time as well. Many studies have concluded that SSR time is not particularly effective. Perhaps SSR's ineffectiveness is due to a lack of accountability and the fact that teachers are reading silently instead of working with students. What's different about Reading Workshop is that teachers spend the self-selected reading time conferring with students, and students often produce written or oral responses to what they read.

TIME TO READ ● Many reading programs devote large blocks of time to instruction and require numerous activities to be completed in centers throughout the week. But they don't give kids time to read, read, read! Research studies have established a direct correlation between time spent reading and improvement in reading skills, yet most classrooms seldom provide even a twenty-minute block of time during the day for silent reading. The Reading Workshop approach gives students at least thirty minutes each day to read independently in the classroom.

Individual Reading Conferences

Another key component of Reading Workshop is the individual teacher-led reading conference. Each day you'll confer with five or six students individually for about five minutes each. You'll ask them questions about what they're reading at home and in the classroom, and you'll guide them to choose a variety of increasingly more challenging books. During the reading conference you become a coach and connect with your students as readers.

Response to Reading

Responding to reading can take many forms, oral and written. It can be a simple book chat with a reading buddy. At other times, the reading response can take the form of a letter, a journal entry, or a graphic organizer. On rare occasions, students may respond with a project or a skit.

But beware of "projectitis"—the tendency to assign so many exciting activities that students spend more time creating projects than they do reading books! Don't forget that every hour spent working on a project is one less hour your students will spend reading. Find a balance that feels right.

Resist the urge to assign book reports and reading projects with the intention of having students "prove" they are reading. Instead, let the response to reading be a genuine attempt to deepen understanding or explore new concepts and connections.

The One-Hour Reading Workshop Session

How do these five components fit together in an hour of reading instruction?

Usually the first fifteen to twenty minutes are spent reading aloud to the class, and the mini-lesson is often part of that read-aloud session. Then students take out their books for self-selected reading time, and they are encouraged to use the mini-lesson strategy in their own reading. One by one, they grab a pillow or folding chair and find a cozy spot in the room to read. For the next thirty to thirty-five minutes, students become immersed in their books and the teacher conducts whispered conferences. After they read, the Reading Workshop closes with students responding to what they have just read by jotting comments in a journal or completing part of a graphic organizer.

READING WORKSHOP SESSION:

- 15 - 20 minutes: Read aloud and mini-lesson
- 30 - 35 minutes: Independent reading and teacher conferences with students
- 10 minutes: Closure activity for responding to reading

Power Reading Tools

Once you have established the basic Reading Workshop, it's time to add the Power Reading Tools. These twelve tools add new components that give focus, direction, and individual accountability to the Reading Workshop program. They are designed to motivate and challenge your students and will empower them to become better readers.

Whether or not you describe strategies as "Power Reading Tools" to your students is up to you. However, if you refer to them this way, make sure your students understand that "power reading" is not synonymous with "speed reading." Reading faster won't necessarily make you a better reader. The objective is not to read faster, but rather, to read more carefully and with greater depth of insight and understanding. They will become power readers, but they won't necessarily become speed readers.

Goal Setting, Record Keeping, and Assessment

In a Power Reading Workshop, you'll challenge your students to set reading goals for themselves and to track their own progress. As a result, they'll become conscious, deliberate readers who take responsibility for reading increasingly more difficult books in a wider variety of genres.

To manage the goal-setting component, each student will need to set up a Power Reading Log. This is as simple as a pocket folder with pages inserted in the middle, and it serves as the organizational system for the whole program. Students will use the Power Reading Log to store their reading response journals, graphic organizers, book genre records, and other literacy materials.

Your students will also evaluate their own progress every few weeks to ensure that they are on track to achieve their goals. In addition, you can administer your own reading assessments, such as quarterly benchmark tests, to make sure that they are making adequate progress according to grade level standards and expectations.

Flexible Guided Reading Groups

Individual conferences are extremely important in the beginning stages of the program, but they have one serious drawback: time constraints. When you confer with each student individually, your conferences must be brief or you will never have time to confer with everyone. Many students need more explicit, small-group reading instruction. To provide this level of reading support, the Power Reading Workshop includes flexible guided reading groups that meet regularly to work with you on specific skills and strategies.

Extended Literary Response

Another way to add depth to the basic Reading Workshop is to offer more reading response options. Several Power Reading Tools offer ways for your students to respond to what they are reading, such as journals, book sharing letters, and graphic organizers. Adding special events such as the Book Buzz and the Magazine Power Hour also increase opportunities for sharing and discussing literature.

Strategic Planning

The first ten days to implement a basic Reading Workshop are completely outlined for you in a step-by-step manner. In addition, the Power Reading Tools are described in detail for you to include as your students become proficient with Reading Workshop. But then what?

Never fear! The Strategic Planning Tool describes how you, the teacher, can take your Reading Workshop to the next level. It provides a clear, easy-to-implement plan for creating powerful reading lessons.

Now you're ready to launch your own Reading Workshop. Start with the basic program, then add the Power Reading Tools. I'll be with you every step of the way...

• • • • • • • • •

CHAPTER 2

Teacher Preparation

TEACHER PREPARATION

• • • • • • • • •

Similar to planning a trip, starting a Reading Workshop requires some advance teacher preparation. Before you start your vacation, you read travel guides, gather important materials, and map out your journey. Implementing your Reading Workshop will also involve several steps to get ready. Consider this guide the "GPS" that will make your journey through Reading Workshop easier.

Here are the three steps you need to do to prepare for your Reading Workshop:

● **STEP 1**: Prepare Reading Workshop materials
● **STEP 2**: Set up your Conference Notebook
● **STEP 3**: Locate and preview Read-Aloud selections

STEP 1 Prepare Reading Workshop Materials

Duplicate the forms you need to get started. At first, students can keep the worksheets in a plain manila file folder, but in a few weeks you'll want to create a more permanent Power Reading Log, using a plastic pocket folder with paper fasteners. This folder will be used for storing reading logs, graphic organizers, and self-assessment materials. It's a critical management component.

The items below are listed in the order you might want to introduce them to your students. After students complete them, be sure to save them for their Power Reading Logs. You can find each of these forms on the pages noted below. Refer to the Materials for the First Ten Days chart on page 29 to determine when you'll need each item.

Student Activity Pages for the First Ten Days:

- **READING INTEREST SURVEY** (page 42) – one for each student

- **MY READING RECORD CHART** (page 48) – start with one for each student—you'll need more later

- **BOOK NOTES** (page 57) – four for each student for the first month of Reading Workshop

- **BOOK GENRE RESPONSE CARDS** (page 66) – one set for each team

- **BOOK GENRE QUESTIONNAIRE** (page 69) – one for each student

MATERIALS FOR THE FIRST TEN DAYS

DAY	LESSON TOPIC	MATERIALS◆	PAGE
1	Getting to Know Your Students	• Reading Interest Surveys • Classroom library or collection of books	40
2	What's Reading Workshop?	• Reading Workshop Guidelines • Chart paper or interactive whiteboard	43
3	Learning to Choose Books	• Chart paper or interactive whiteboard • My Reading Record forms	46
4	Conferring with Students	• Teacher's Conference Notebook	49
5	Reading Is Thinking	• Chart paper or interactive whiteboard • Sticky notes	51
6	Written Response to Reading	• Book Notes forms • Reading Reflections forms (optional)	55
7	More Thinking about Reading	• Reading Is Thinking chart from Day 5 • Book Notes forms	60
8	Fiction or Nonfiction?	• 15 to 20 books of different genres • Basal readers (optional)	62
9	Identifying Book Genres	• 15 to 20 books from Day 8 • Book Genre Response cards • Chart paper or interactive whiteboard	64
10	Identifying Genre Preferences	• Book Genre Response cards • Book Genre Questionnaires	67

◆ Every day you'll need a short read-aloud book appropriate for the day's lesson. Refer to the read-aloud suggestions on page 35.

STEP 2 Teacher's Conference Notebook

You will start conferring with students once you have established good classroom control during the individual reading time in your Reading Workshop. You will confer with each student individually at least once a week. When you confer, it is important to keep accurate anecdotal records. The Conference Notebook is an organized system for recording your observations.

Set Up Your Conference Notebook

Use a three-ring binder for your Conference Notebook. Put at least one copy of the Individual Reading Conference Record (page 31) in the notebook for each student and write one student's name on each page. Organize them in alphabetical order and place them in the notebook. Each page provides enough room for three weeks' worth of notes. You may also want to keep the Questions for Conferring (page 32) in the front of the binder for your own reference.

When and How to Begin Conferring

Wait until your Reading Workshop is running smoothly before you start conferring with students individually. Make sure your students are able to follow the Reading Workshop guidelines and that most of them can settle down and read silently for at least fifteen to twenty minutes. If you begin working with individuals before you resolve classroom management issues, you risk having your quiet workshop environment become noisy and chaotic.

When you're ready to start conferences, let your students know you'll be meeting with them individually to discuss their books. Limit your discussion with each student to one question or set of related questions. Keep each conference short so that you can meet with all your students during the week. Record notes about each conference before moving to the next student.

Name: _____

INDIVIDUAL READING CONFERENCE RECORD

Week of: _____ Mon   Tues   Wed   Thurs   Fri

Title/Type of Reading Material: _____

Comments/Observations: _____

_____

_____

_____

- -

Week of: _____ Mon   Tues   Wed   Thurs   Fri

Title/Type of Reading Material: _____

Comments/Observations: _____

_____

_____

_____

- -

Week of: _____ Mon   Tues   Wed   Thurs   Fri

Title/Type of Reading Material: _____

Comments/Observations: _____

_____

_____

_____

QUESTIONS FOR CONFERRING

Choose one of these questions or sets of questions to discuss with each student during your individual reading conference. Feel free to add your own questions as well.

- Why did you choose this book? Is it easy, just right, or challenging? Explain.

- Would you recommend this book to someone else? Who would like this book? Why?

- Describe your favorite part in this book. Why is it your favorite part?

- Was there something in the book that you didn't understand?

- Which part of the book made you want to ask a question?

- How can you connect this book to something in your own life?

- How does the book remind you of other books you've read?

- If you were the author, how would you have written the book differently?

- What part would you change? Why?

- How did you feel while reading this book? Did you feel happy, sad, excited, etc? Explain.

- Which character in this book most appeals to you? Why does this character appeal to you? How can you relate?

- Have you learned any fun or interesting vocabulary words to add to your personal word wall or to our class wall?

- What questions do you still have? Where could you find the answers to those questions?

- What words did you notice in the book that you didn't know? How did you figure out those words' meanings?

- What character traits describe the main character? What clues helped you identify those traits?

- Describe what you visualized as you read a portion of the book.

- Summarize the most important event in this book so far. Why did you pick this event?

- Make a prediction as to what will happen next. What textual evidence supports your prediction?

♦ Thanks to the Joyful Reading Discussion Group who compiled this list of teacher questions.

STEP 3 Locate and Preview Books

Reading aloud to your class is one of the key elements of the Reading Workshop approach, and something you'll do at virtually every Reading Workshop session.

Review the Ten Days of Read Alouds chart on page 35. Look at each lesson topic and the book choices available. Choose one of these books for each lesson, or another book you are familiar with that is appropriate for the topic.

Review the following tips for reading aloud to gain confidence in your ability to read to your class.

Tips for Reading Aloud

- Preview books to decide if they are suitable for the lesson and for your students.

- As you preview each book, mark places in the book that may work for "think alouds" or skill lessons.

- Choose books that you enjoy. If you don't like a book, you won't be able to convince your students that you do.

- Since mini-lessons should be short, you may want to read the book over several days or substitute an article or basal reader story.

- If prior knowledge of specific concepts is necessary for understanding, introduce those ideas before reading the book. Use Google Earth to show locations or historical images to recreate times and places.

- Read aloud with expression and enthusiasm. Don't be afraid that you will sound silly by reading the story dramatically. Your students will love it!

- Consider using the same short book several times for different mini-lessons. Read the book aloud one time for enjoyment. The next time you read it, use it for a mini-lesson such as character development. Then read the book later in the year and use it for a different skill or strategy. Because students are familiar with the book, they can focus on how the skill or strategy applies to the story.

- If appropriate, let student volunteers read aloud the character parts. For this strategy, you'll need multiple copies of the same read-aloud book. Choose one student for each main character and tell them which pages you plan to read. Allow them a few minutes to review their parts, and then read the selection aloud to the class. You will read all the narration, but when it's time for a character to speak, he or she will stand up and do so with expression.

- If you have a document camera, place the book under the camera and project it so that your students can follow along with you. However, be aware that they may read ahead so you might want to keep part of the page covered.

- If you don't have a document camera, you may be able to purchase a Kindle version of the book instead. Amazon.com has a free Kindle reader that you can download to any computer and use to read Kindle books. With the aid of a projector, you can display the Kindle copy on a whiteboard or screen so your students can follow along. You can also highlight text and use other Kindle reading features.

Laura's Tips

Make a copy of the Ten Days of Read Alouds chart (page 35) to take with you to your school's Media Center. If you plan in advance, you may be able to give the chart to the school librarian, who can pull the books from the shelves for you. If your Media Center doesn't have some of the books, the librarian may be able to recommend suitable replacements.

Ten Days of Read Alouds

DAY	LESSON TOPIC	READ-ALOUD OPTIONS♦
1	Getting to Know Your Students	• *Thank You, Mr. Falker* ~ Polacco • *Teacher from the Black Lagoon* ~ Thaler
2	What's Reading Workshop?	• *Crickwing* ~ Cannon • *The Rainbow Fish* ~ Pfister
3	Learning to Choose Books	• *Goldie Socks and the Three Libearians* ~ Hopkins • *We're Going on a Book Hunt* ~ Miller
4	Conferring with Students	• *Chrysanthemum* ~ Henkes • *Have You Filled a Bucket Today?* ~ McCloud
5	Reading Is Thinking	• *The Train to Somewhere* ~ Bunting • *The Wretched Stone* ~ Van Allsburg
6	Written Response to Reading	• *The Diary of a Worm* ~ Cronin • *Enemy Pie* ~ Munson
7	More Thinking about Reading	• *The True Story of the Three Little Pigs* ~ Scieszka • *Tuesday* ~ Weisner
8	Fiction or Nonfiction?	• *Stellaluna* ~ Cannon • *Bats* ~ Gibbons
9	Identifying Book Genres	• *A Writing Kind of Day* ~ Fletcher • *Random House Book of Poetry for Children* ~ Prelutsky
10	Identifying Genre Preferences	• *Wilma Unlimited* ~ Krull • *The Kid Who Invented the Popsicle* ~ Wulffson

♦ Choose one of these books for each lesson or another book that is appropriate for the lesson topic. Each title is followed by the author's last name. Preview books to determine grade level suitability. A full annotated bibliography of these books starts on page 137.

• • • • • • • • • •

CHAPTER 3

Basic Reading Workshop

BASIC READING WORKSHOP
• • • • • • • • • •

How you introduce the Reading Workshop approach to your students will depend on how long you have been working with them. The plan described below assumes that you are starting on the first day of school; it may need to be adapted if you are starting in the middle of the school year. It may also need to be adapted according to your own comfort level with this approach. This section explains how to get started with a very basic Reading Workshop model; you'll add the "power" components as your students become ready for them.

Daily Reading Workshop Structure

Begin by establishing a regular Reading Workshop routine in your classroom. Many teachers use the following structure:

- Read aloud and mini-lesson: 15 to 20 minutes
- Independent reading and conferring: 30 to 35 minutes
- Closure or response to reading: 10 minutes

The ten lesson ideas in this chapter will help you establish this structure over the next two weeks. The Reading Workshop approach may be completely foreign to your students, so they may need time to adjust to each part of the workshop. The first few lessons won't adhere to this format because it takes time to introduce the individual parts of the Reading Workshop, but over the next few weeks you will work toward establishing the three-part structure described above.

Remember that for each of the first ten lessons, you'll need to choose a book that can be read aloud in one sitting. Carefully select each book for the particular purpose described in the lesson. Each lesson includes two suggested book titles that would work well, and you can find the entire list of suggestions on page 35. Later you can begin reading chapter books aloud and creating your own mini-lessons based on the content of those books.

Please note that while this section is organized into ten individual days, you might actually spend as much as a month establishing your basic Reading Workshop. Take as much time as you need. Since it's important to allow students time for independent reading every single day, you may need to take several days to teach some mini-lessons. Don't worry! Quality instruction is more important than sticking to a timeline, and rushing through a lesson will only leave you and your students feeling stressed. Relax and enjoy the journey!

DAY 1 Getting to Know Your Students

As you implement a Reading Workshop in your classroom, you'll connect with your students in amazing ways. The Reading Interest Survey will help you assess their feelings about reading before they embark on the Reading Workshop journey with you. It's also important to give them time to read on their own the very first day. Finally, end by reading aloud one of your favorite books. Following these simple steps will give your students a taste of the Reading Workshop experience, leaving them eager for more.

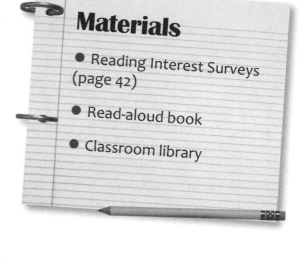

Materials
- Reading Interest Surveys (page 42)
- Read-aloud book
- Classroom library

Suggested Read Alouds
- *Thank You, Mr. Falker* ~ Polacco
- *Teacher from the Black Lagoon* ~ Thaler

Reading Survey

Begin by asking your students to take a survey that will help you understand their reading preferences. Be sure to administer it before discussing your reading program with them. If you wait too long, your students may not respond honestly if they dislike reading. Simply pass out the survey and tell them you want to learn more about each of them as readers. If you're planning to allow students to check out books from your classroom library on Day 1, briefly review your guidelines for doing so. Then, as the class completes the survey, allow small groups of students to visit your classroom library to select a book.

READING INTEREST SURVEY

Name _____ Date _____

How do you feel about reading? Be honest! Explain your feelings.

What do you like about reading?

What don't you like about reading?

Do you have a favorite series? If so, what is it and why do you like it?

Do you ever read at home just for fun, even when you aren't required to read? If so, what types of things do you enjoy reading?

What topics would you like to read about this year?

Do you like to read newspapers or magazines? Explain.

Independent Reading

Encourage students to read silently until everyone finishes their surveys. Limit movement around the room on Day 1 since you haven't yet discussed guidelines for choosing a location in the room to read. The students will finish their surveys at different times, so some will have more time for independent reading than others, but try to make sure they all have a little time to read on the first day. While they are reading, start to notice your students' preferences. Who heads for the fiction books? Who grabs a nonfiction book? What are they reading about? Are they engrossed in their books or do they seem to have difficulty concentrating?

Read Aloud

After you collect the surveys, introduce your students to the joys of listening to a great book. One of my favorite read alouds for the first day is *Thank You, Mr. Falker* because it's short enough to be read in one setting and it touches on important issues. The author, Patricia Polacco, writes from her own experience about having trouble learning to read and the humiliation of being bullied. By introducing this theme on the first day of school, you set a positive expectation for success in reading. Once again, use this as an opportunity to learn about your students as readers and listeners. Do they seem to enjoy the read-aloud session? Who participates actively by asking questions or making connections with their own experiences? Does anyone seem disinterested or disengaged? No need to take any other action right now; just observe and begin to learn about your students.

Closure

Wrap up Day 1 by explaining that tomorrow you'll have some exciting news for them about how they will learn to become better readers in your classroom. If they haven't found a good book to read from your classroom library, ask them to bring a book from home.

Laura's Tips

For a more detailed interest survey, use the Activities and Interests chart found in the Appendix on pages 130 and 131. This two-page chart allows students to rate several dozen activities from 1 to 5 to indicate their preferences.

READING INTEREST SURVEY

Name _____ Date _____

How do you feel about reading? Be honest! Explain your feelings.

_____

_____

_____

_____

What do you like about reading?

_____

_____

What don't you like about reading?

_____

_____

Do you have a favorite series? If so, what is it and why do you like it?

_____

_____

_____

Do you ever read at home just for fun, even when you aren't required to read?
If so, what types of things do you enjoy reading?

_____

_____

What topics would you like to read about this year?

_____

_____

Do you like to read newspapers or magazines? Explain.

_____

_____

DAY 2 What's Reading Workshop?

You've already begun to set the stage for Reading Workshop by surveying your students, reading aloud, and giving them time to read independently. Today you'll introduce the term "Reading Workshop," along with a general overview of how the program works. Then you and your students will create guidelines for their participation during independent reading.

Materials

- Read-aloud book
- Chart paper or whiteboard
- Reading Workshop Guidelines

Suggested Read Alouds
- *Crickwing* ~ Cannon
- *The Rainbow Fish* ~ Pfister

Getting Started

Begin by asking your students how they would feel if they could choose their own books and have time to read at school every day. If they've never been exposed to the Reading Workshop approach, they might be amazed at the very thought! No reading textbook? No daily worksheets? No reading kits? Explain that your classroom will become a "Reading Workshop" where you'll read aloud every day and they'll read their own books.

Read Aloud

Next, read aloud a short book that conveys strong visual images or one that allows students to make connections. *Crickwing* and *The Rainbow Fish* are good selections for making connections, and several of the resources in the Appendix offer other options. Read with enthusiasm and expression, but don't try to engage them in too many "think alouds" during this session. You'll be able to refer to the book in future lessons, but just let the students enjoy listening today.

Mini-lesson: Establishing Guidelines

Before beginning your independent reading time today, explain that you know that some of them would be more comfortable reading in another location in the classroom. However, it's important to keep the room very quiet and to avoid distractions so that everyone is able to concentrate on reading. Ask students to suggest guidelines for behavior that will help everyone respect each other's rights no matter where they are sitting. Create a poster or chart of guidelines and plan to review it each day for the first few days. You can use the ideas on page 45 as suggestions to include on the class chart.

READING WORKSHOP GUIDELINES

- Take care of personal needs (bathroom and water) before Reading Workshop.

- Choose a reading spot and stay in it.

- Bring enough reading material to your spot to keep you reading the whole time.

- Remain quiet and respect the rights of others around you.

- Get lost in your book!

Independent Reading

After establishing the guidelines, be sure to allow at least twenty minutes for independent reading. If you aren't comfortable allowing all of your students to move away from their desks, let half choose a special spot and keep the others at their desks, letting them know that their roles will be reversed the next day. Monitor your students' behavior, and if you find that some of them have forgotten the guidelines, quietly ask them to return to their seats for the remainder of reading class.

Don't try to do too much in the way of conferring with readers today; just observe what they have selected to read and how they respond to this newfound freedom.

Closure

After the independent reading session is over, ask students to return to their seats. Review the guidelines one more time and ask students if they can think of any rules that should be added or changed.

Laura's Tips

To minimize confusion when students are moving to a new spot, don't let them get up all at once, or there'll be a mad dash for the three pillows and the two carpet squares! I usually put students' names on craft sticks and place them in a cup. Then I draw out a few names at a time until everyone has selected a cozy spot to read.

Reading Workshop Guidelines

- **Take care of personal needs (bathroom and water) before Reading Workshop.**

- **Choose a reading spot and stay in it.**

- **Bring enough reading material to your spot to keep you reading the whole time.**

- **Remain quiet and respect the rights of others around you.**

- **Get lost in your book!**

DAY 3 Learning to Choose Books

Many students have no idea how to find a good book on their own. The first time I asked my class how to find a good book, their overwhelming response was to look at the Accelerated Reader (AR) points or to look for a certain color reading level sticker. When I asked them what they would do in a library or store that didn't have AR labels, they were baffled! Most students have never been taught how to select a "just right" book, so it's critical that we introduce these strategies now.

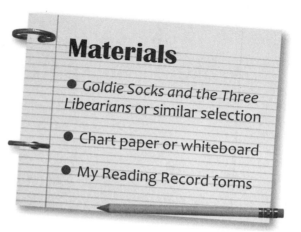

Materials

● *Goldie Socks and the Three Libearians* or similar selection

● Chart paper or whiteboard

● My Reading Record forms

Suggested Read Alouds
● *Goldie Socks and the Three Libearians* ~ Hopkins
● *We're Going on a Book Hunt* (primary grades) ~ Miller

Before You Begin

If possible, locate the book *Goldie Socks and the Three Libearians* or a similar book to read aloud to your students. In this particular story, Goldie Socks finds a cottage made of books in the woods. Curious, she sneaks in and begins looking for a good book. Some are too easy, some are too hard, and one is just right! She uses the five-finger rule to determine which book is just right for her. This book is wonderful for teaching kids how to choose a good book, and the surprise ending will delight your students. If you can't find this book or something with a similar theme, skip the read-aloud portion of the lesson and focus on strategies for choosing a good book.

Read Aloud & Mini-lesson

Begin today's lesson by asking your students how they find a good book. Discuss the concept of easy, just right, and challenging books. Share with them books from your own life that fit into each category. Let them share their ideas with the class and begin a class chart entitled "How to Find a Just Right Book." If you have located a copy of *Goldie Socks and the Three Libearians*, explain that you want to share a story with them in which the main character uses many strategies to find a good book. Read the book aloud, and ask students to recall the strategies Goldie Socks used in the story. Add those ideas to the chart and any others suggested by your students. These might include looking at the front cover, searching for a favorite author, or reading the blurb on the inside flap.

Independent Reading

Before sending your students off to read, give them a copy of the My Reading Record form and ask them to record the books they are reading independently. Ask them to try the five-finger rule on a few different pages with their own books to see if they're too easy, just right, or too challenging. Tell them not to worry about the *Genre* column at this point.

MY READING RECORD ★ ★	Name						
TITLE	AUTHOR'S LAST NAME	PAGES	LEVEL E, JR, C	DATE STARTED	DATE FINISHED	GENRE(S)	

Level Codes: E = Easy   JR = Just Right   C = Challenging

Closure

After your students finish reading, collect the forms from your students and review them for accuracy. Notice whether they have classified their books as *Easy*, *Just Right*, or *Challenging*. Let them know that it's okay to read books that aren't *just right*, and it's also okay to stop reading a book if you realize you didn't make a good choice. Some students may want to find another book to read before your next reading class.

Laura's Tips

The Five-Finger Rule

Share the five-finger rule with your students. Here's how it works: Open a book to any full page and begin reading. Put your hand on the table in front of you and make a fist. Every time you have difficulty with a word, uncurl one finger. If you uncurl all five fingers before the end of the page, the book is too difficult. If you never uncurl a finger, the book is too easy.

My Reading Record

Name _____

Title	Author's Last Name	Pages	Level E, JR, C	Date Started	Date Finished	Genre(s)

Level Codes: E = Easy   JR = Just Right   C = Challenging

DAY 4 Conferring with Students

By Day 4, you and your students will be starting to feel comfortable with the Reading Workshop routine. They'll know that each day you'll start by reading aloud, and then they will have the opportunity to read independently. When they are able to settle down for at least fifteen to twenty minutes of uninterrupted reading, it's time to begin conferring with students about what they are reading. If they are still having trouble following the guidelines (being ready with a book, staying in one spot, etc.), spend a few more days teaching the routines before you begin meeting with students individually.

Materials

● Short engaging read-aloud book

● Teacher's Conference Notebook (see page 30)

Suggested Read Alouds
● *Chrysanthemum* ~ Henkes
● *Have You Filled a Bucket Today?* ~ McCloud

Before You Begin

Prior to the day's lesson, make a list of the students you want to meet with today. Plan to meet with each student at least once a week, though you may want to meet with struggling readers more frequently. For today, meet with as many of your at-risk students as possible to make sure they have appropriate reading material. You may want to start with students who identified their books as too easy or too challenging on the Reading Record form yesterday.

Read Aloud & Mini-lesson

Begin by reading aloud a short book of your choice, something that you know your students will enjoy. Then explain that today you will start meeting with each of them, one at a time, to discuss what they are reading. Explain that you want to learn more about them as readers and you'll be meeting with just four or five students a day. Show them your Teacher's Conference Notebook and tell them that you might make a few notes while they are talking with you. The notes are just to help you remember what you talked about, and your students aren't being graded on their responses.

Independent Reading & Conferring

Before you begin conferring with students, make sure that they are all settled comfortably into their reading spots with a book. Then quietly call your students, one by one, over to a conference table to sit with you, or sneak around and meet with them where they are reading. Try both methods to see which one feels most comfortable and least disruptive to other readers. To help you manage your time, use a quiet countdown timer and set it for five minutes when you begin meeting with each student.

At first, keep your conferences simple by asking your students what they are reading and why they chose their book. You can also have them whisper-read a part they liked or a few sentences from the book. Make notes on your conference form for each student, but keep your notes private. This record is for your eyes only, though you may decide to share it with parents at a future parent-teacher conference. After you jot a few notes, thank the student and move to the next student on your list. Later in the year, you can use the Questions for Conferring on page 32 to help you confer with them in more meaningful ways.

Closure

When the reading and conferring time is over, have students return to their seats and make sure their Reading Records are up to date. Let them know that if they didn't have a conference with you today, you'll be meeting with them sometime during the next week.

● ● ● ● ● ● ● ●

DAY 5 Reading Is Thinking

Research has shown that simply having students read more is not enough to improve reading skills; students need to be engaged in thinking about their reading. In this lesson, you'll teach students to become more aware of what they are thinking while reading.

Suggested Read Alouds
- *The Train to Somewhere* ~ Bunting
- *The Wretched Stone* ~ Van Allsburg

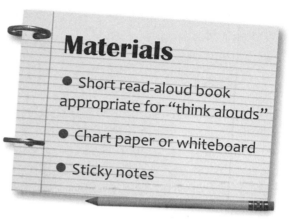

Materials
- Short read-aloud book appropriate for "think alouds"
- Chart paper or whiteboard
- Sticky notes

Read Aloud & Mini-lesson

1 Ask your students, "What is reading?" Usually students say that reading is saying the words in a book, but some students may refer to reading strategies.

2 Explain that "reading is thinking" because good readers use their minds and think while reading. Refer to one of the books you read previously, and give an example of the types of thinking you did while reading. It could be a connection you made, a question you wondered about, or a word you had to decode.

3 Post a sheet of chart paper with the heading "Reading Is Thinking" and ask students what kinds of thinking they do while reading. Jot down their ideas for future reference. For some of the responses you might expect, see the sample responses on page 54.

4 Read aloud a short book that allows you to demonstrate your thinking. Stop a few times while reading to think aloud about what you are thinking while reading. In particular, refer to the items on the class chart and show how you are using those strategies. Allow students to add more items to the chart as you read.

Independent Reading & Conferring

Before you students move to their reading locations, ask them to notice the kinds of thinking they do today when they read their own books independently. Give them at least twenty minutes for reading and have them record one type of thinking on at least two different sticky notes. Ask them to save their sticky notes to share with you during a future conference. As you confer with each student, discuss the kinds of thinking they are doing while reading.

Closure

If your students are ready, try a partner activity for closure today. Assign book buddies, and have them turn and talk to their buddy about the types of thinking they were doing while reading. However, introduce this step only when they are ready for this type of interaction. If your students have not developed the social skills needed for a productive partner discussion, save this step for later.

LAURA'S Tips

Don't let any mini-lesson take up the entire reading block. If you sense that your students are restless during the mini-lesson, stop for the day and continue the lesson the next day. Be sure to allow at least twenty to thirty minutes for independent reading every day. Your students look forward to this special time.

Reading Is Thinking

READING IS THINKING
SAMPLE

When we read we...

- Make movies in our minds about what's happening in the book

- Make predictions about what might happen next

- Notice how the characters behave and think as we do

- Ask questions about parts we don't understand

- Reread parts we don't understand to clear up confusion

- Try to figure out new words based on context clues

DAY 6 Written Response to Reading

Having students jot down a few notes about what they are reading each day provides the teacher with a rich source of information about their reading habits. However, many students are turned off by writing lengthy journal responses every day. The Book Notes form is a perfect response tool. It's concise, yet provides important data about your students' reading habits.

Suggested Read Alouds
- *The Diary of a Worm* ~ Cronin
- *Enemy Pie* ~ Munson

Read Aloud & Mini-lesson

Introduce the Book Notes form to students by explaining that it's a simple way for them to record a little bit about what they are reading each day. You can ask students to respond on their Book Notes form in a variety of ways, but at first you may want them to begin with a simple summary of what they have read. To model that skill, read aloud a short book that's easy to summarize. Then ask students to practice writing a short summary of the book's plot. Move about the room so you can see what they are writing, and choose a few clear examples to read aloud to the class.

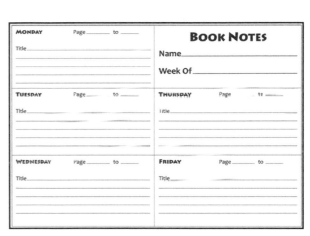

Independent Reading & Conferring

Distribute one copy of the Book Notes form to each student and have each complete the name and date information. Then have each student write his/her book title and starting page number in today's block. Students may only move to their reading location after they have completed this step each day.

Closure

Allow five or ten minutes for students to write their ending page number and a few sentences about what they have just read. Collect the Book Notes each day and review them before returning them to your students the next day. You'll be amazed at the insights you'll glean from this simple process!

LAURA'S **Tips**

You may want to use the Book Notes form as a way to hold students accountable for their participation during Independent Reading. If so, consider the assessment ideas that follow on page 58.

BOOK NOTES

Name _____

Week Of _____

MONDAY

Title _____

Page _____ to _____

_____

_____

_____

_____

TUESDAY

Title _____

Page _____ to _____

_____

_____

_____

_____

WEDNESDAY

Title _____

Page _____ to _____

_____

_____

_____

_____

THURSDAY

Title _____

Page _____ to _____

_____

_____

_____

_____

FRIDAY

Title _____

Page _____ to _____

_____

_____

_____

_____

Assessment Ideas for Book Notes

Should you use the Book Notes form to assess performance during reading? That's a decision only you can make. Many teachers like using the form without having to assign a grade; others are required to obtain weekly grades and find that the Book Notes form is a quick and easy assessment tool.

One way is to have students assess their own performance. Post the Reading Reflections questions (page 59) and ask students to secretly jot down the answer to each question. By counting the number of *yes* and *no* responses, they can obtain a score for that day's performance. Ask them to jot down the appropriate letter (*E*, *S*, *N*, or *U*) in the block for that day on their Book Notes form. Then ask them to think about the reflection questions at the bottom of the page. For students who earned an *N* or a *U*, it might help to have them respond to those questions in writing on the back of the Book Notes form.

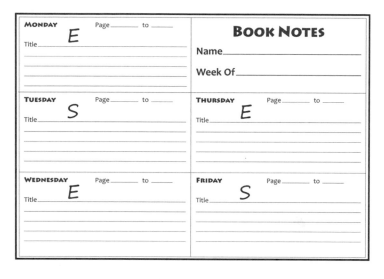

Collect the forms to make sure you agree with their self-assessment scores. If not, discuss your own assessment with those students. Be sure to note on the form why you don't agree with their assessment. At the end of the week, review each student's overall performance and assign an appropriate letter grade as shown below.

You can also convert the responses to a point system. Simply have each student record the number of *yes* answers each day on their Book Notes form. With 5 points possible each day, they can earn a maximum of 25 points for the week. Multiply the total by 4 to convert this score to a 100-point scale. For example, a student who earned 23 points would earn 92 for the week.

LAURA'S Tips

Sometimes students who move away from their desks to read have trouble focusing. They are easily distracted by other students or items in the classroom. If this is true in your classroom, establish a rule that students must earn a minimum score of 4 points in order to be granted this freedom the following day.

READING REFLECTIONS

How did you do during Reading Workshop today?

1 Were you ready with your books and/or materials at the start of the workshop?

2 Did you select reading materials that are just right or challenging?

3 Did you move quickly to your reading spot and stay in it the whole time?

4 Were you reading the entire time?

5 Did you complete your Book Notes form or written response correctly?

Find your score:

All Yes	=	E (Excellent)
4 Yes/1 No	=	S (Satisfactory)
3 Yes/2 No	=	N (Needs improvement)
Mostly No	=	U (Unsatisfactory)

Reflect:

Do you need to improve?
If so, what will you do differently next time?

DAY 7 More Thinking about Reading

Now that you've introduced the daily Book Notes activity, it's time to revisit the Reading Is Thinking discussion you started on Day 5. Feel free to spend several days developing this concept. Some teachers like to devote one or more days to each individual type of thinking, such as visualizing, questioning, predicting, making connections, and so on.

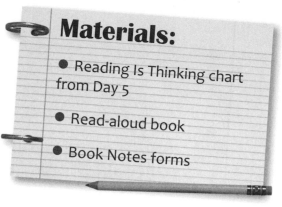

Materials:

● Reading Is Thinking chart from Day 5

● Read-aloud book

● Book Notes forms

Suggested Read Alouds
● *The True Story of the Three Little Pigs* ~ Scieszka
● *Tuesday* ~ Weisner

Read Aloud & Mini-lesson

Post the chart that lists the types of thinking that good readers do when reading. Ask if anyone has thought of any additional strategies to add to the list. Read aloud another short book that will allow you to model various types of thinking about reading. Begin by asking students to make predictions about the story based on its author, title, and cover. As you read, stop to model the kinds of thinking you are doing. For example, if a part of the book makes you wonder about something, voice your question aloud. Or if you read an unfamiliar word, stop to discuss how the context clues helped you figure out the word's meaning.

> **READING IS THINKING**
> SAMPLE
> When we read we...
>
> ● Make movies in our minds about what's happening in the book
>
> ● Make predictions about what might happen next
>
> ● Notice how the characters behave and think as we do
>
> ● Ask questions about parts we don't understand
>
> ● Reread parts we don't understand to clear up confusion
>
> ● Try to figure out new words based on context clues

Independent Reading & Conferring

Remember to distribute the Book Notes form before they begin reading independently. Have them write their titles and starting pages on the form before they move to a new location to read. Confer with four or five more students today, and refer to their Book Notes during your conference. Ask them to tell you what they are thinking while reading, and use the Reading Is Thinking chart or the Questions for Conferring list to prompt them.

Closing Activity

Instead of asking students to write a summary on their Book Notes forms, ask them to write about what they were thinking while reading. It could have been a connection, a question, or a prediction. If they aren't sure what to write, they may write a summary as usual. Once again, collect the forms and review them.

LAURA'S Tips

Remember that if you have a document camera in your classroom, you can use it during your read-aloud sessions. Students can often make inferences and predictions by looking at the pictures and the text. However, you'll want to keep a cover sheet handy so you can hide pictures or text that might give away parts of the story too early!

• • • • • • • • •

DAY 8 Fiction or Nonfiction?

Teaching students to identify book genres can help them find books they like to read. However, before students can identify book genres, they should be able to classify books as fiction or nonfiction. Today you'll shorten your read-aloud session to allow time for an activity that demonstrates the difference between fiction and nonfiction books.

Suggested Read Alouds
- *Stellaluna* ~ Cannon
- *Bats* ~ Gibbons

Materials:
- 15 to 20 books that span a variety of genres and include both fiction and nonfiction
- Basal readers (optional)

Before You Begin

Prior to this lesson, gather at least fifteen different books that span a variety of genres and include both fiction and nonfiction. Locate two books on the same topic, where one is a fiction book and the other is nonfiction. *Stellaluna* and *Bats* work well because they are both about bats, but *Stellaluna* is clearly a work of fiction. If your school has a set of basal reader textbooks, these can also be used for the lesson, but they aren't necessary.

Read Aloud & Mini-lesson

Start the lesson by asking your class if they know the difference between fiction and nonfiction. As students respond, lead the class to a deeper understanding of these two broad categories. Show the books *Stellaluna* and *Bats*, and read aloud just enough of both books for students to see that while the subject matter of both is bats, one is fiction and one is nonfiction. Discuss the characteristics of each book that help with their classification. Many students aren't aware that biographies, folklore, and poetry are examples of nonfiction. Use one of the two activity ideas below to test their understanding of fiction and nonfiction.

Activity 1: Is It Nonfiction?

1 One at a time, hold up different books in a variety of genres.

2 If they think the book is nonfiction, they are to show you a thumbs-up sign.

3 If it's fiction, they point their thumbs down.

4 Go through the set of books quickly, discussing and clarifying as needed.

LAURA'S Tips

Another way to get a quick group response is to use response cards instead of the thumbs-up/thumbs-down strategy. For the "Is It Nonfiction?" activity, have students label index cards with the word *fiction* on one side and *nonfiction* on the other and show them to you as you hold up each book.

Activity 2: Fiction or Nonfiction Hunt

1 If your students have basal reading texts, ask them to work with a partner to find examples of fiction and nonfiction selections.

2 Randomly call on students to name a selection and classify it as fiction or nonfiction.

3 Ask members of the class to give details to support or challenge the classification.

Independent Reading

As students begin their independent reading, ask them to hunt for evidence that will enable them to classify their book as fiction or nonfiction.

Closure

At the end of class, ask students to write on their Book Notes form whether their book is fiction or nonfiction and their reasons for classifying it that way. Ask a few volunteers to share their book titles and classifications with the class. Be sure to finish reading *Stellaluna* later that day or the next day because it's a wonderful story with a friendship theme. If you don't have time to read *Bats* to the whole class, make it available during independent reading time for students who are interested in learning more about bats.

DAY 9 Identifying Book Genres

If your students need more help distinguishing between fiction and nonfiction, spend an extra day on that lesson before you teach them to identify specific book genres.

Suggested Read Alouds
- *A Writing Kind of Day* ~ Fletcher
- *The Random House Book of Poetry for Children* ~ Prelutsky

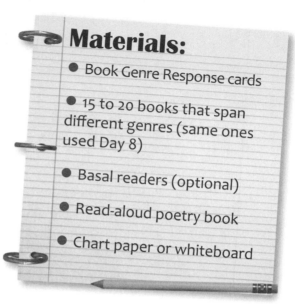

Materials:
- Book Genre Response cards
- 15 to 20 books that span different genres (same ones used Day 8)
- Basal readers (optional)
- Read-aloud poetry book
- Chart paper or whiteboard

Before You Begin

Divide the class into teams of three to four students. Duplicate a set of Book Genre Response cards for each team and cut them apart. Gather a variety of books of different genres and examine your basal reading text for examples to use in this lesson. Choose two or three poems to read in Step 1 of your mini-lesson.

Read Aloud & Mini-lesson

1 For your read-aloud session today, read and discuss a few poems. Then explain that the categories of fiction and nonfiction are very broad, and books are further classified into more specific categories called "genres."

2 Use the poetry book as an example of the poetry genre and ask them if they can name other book genres. As students respond, write the genres on chart paper or the board. Be sure to explain the characteristics of each genre as you add it to the chart. Mention examples of books the students may have already read that fit each genre category or offer suggestions from the basal reader.

3 Be sure that you have discussed all the genres in the Book Genre Response cards. If students leave out any important genres, mention them yourself and explain their characteristics.

4 Use the "think and touch" strategy to check for understanding. Give each team a set of Book Genre Response cards and ask them to spread the cards out face up. Hold up a book or display a selection from the basal reader and describe it briefly. Ask everyone to think about how they would classify the book or selection. On the count of three, have them touch the appropriate genre card. If they touch different cards, have them discuss the reasons for their choices and come to a team consensus. Quickly check each team's choice before moving on to the next book.

BOOK GENRE RESPONSE CARDS	
Informational	Biography
Poetry	Folklore
Historical Fiction	Science Fiction
Fantasy	Mystery
Adventure	Realistic Fiction

Independent Reading & Conferring

Give students the remainder of the class period to read independently. As you confer with students, begin looking at their Reading Records and discussing genre with them.

Closure

At the end of class have the students show their books to their team members and classify each book according to genre, giving details from the book to support their choice. Then ask students to take out their Reading Record forms and classify each of the books they have read so far according to its specific genre.

LAURA'S Tips

Point out that genres are subcategories of the broader classifications of fiction and nonfiction. Some genres are obviously one or the other, but others like poetry and folklore are not so easily classified. Both of those genres are considered nonfiction despite the fact that they often tell a story.

BOOK GENRE RESPONSE CARDS

Informational	Biography
Poetry	Folklore
Historical Fiction	Science Fiction
Fantasy	Mystery
Adventure	Realistic Fiction

DAY 10 Identifying Genre Preferences

Your students should now have a better understanding of the many types of books available, but do you know what *they* prefer? This lesson will help you help them identify their book preferences. Ultimately, this will assist you in guiding them to find "just right" books.

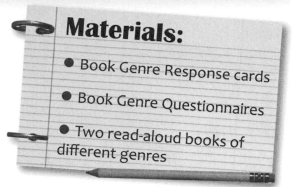

Materials:

● Book Genre Response cards

● Book Genre Questionnaires

● Two read-aloud books of different genres

Suggested Read Alouds
● *Wilma Unlimited* ~ Krull
● *The Kid Who Invented the Popsicle* ~ Wulffson

Before You Begin

Find two books of different genres that you can use for demonstration purposes. *Wilma Unlimited* is a biography and *The Kid Who Invented the Popsicle* is informational, but you can choose any two books you like. A science fiction book and a science informational book on a similar topic would be a particularly effective pair. Students frequently confuse science fiction with informational books on science topics.

Read Aloud & Mini-lesson

1 Begin with a quick review of the previous day's genre lesson. Hold up each Book Genre Response card one at a time. Ask students to turn to a partner and discuss the characteristics of that genre. If time allows, ask them to name at least one familiar example of that genre.

2 Next, read aloud a few pages from the two books of different genres you selected earlier. Ask students to identify the genre of each book and discuss any text features that served as clues to that genre.

3 Then distribute the Book Genre Questionnaire and explain that you would like to learn more about the kinds of books your students enjoy. Guide them through the questionnaire, one genre at a time.

4 For each genre they select on the list, they should give at least one example of a book they've read or a topic in that genre that interests them. For example, under *Nonfiction – Science* they might list animals, rocks, chemistry, or robots.

Independent Reading & Conferring

As students finish their surveys, allow them to move to their favorite reading spots. If some students have difficulty completing the genre survey on their own, tell them you'll work with them to complete it during their next conference. Continue conferring with individual students and discussing their genre preferences with them throughout the week.

Closure

After students finish reading for the day, have them discuss their surveys with a book buddy. They can talk over their favorite genres and books they've read from those genres. Collect the surveys and save them to read and discuss during your next conference with each student.

BOOK GENRE QUESTIONNAIRE

Name _____ Date _____

Which of the following types of books do you like? For each type of book that you like, try to think of an example or a specific topic. This will assist me in helping you find more great books!

Nonfiction   Examples of Topics or Books You Like

- ☐ Biographies _____
- ☐ Science _____
- ☐ History _____
- ☐ Poetry _____
- ☐ Supernatural _____
- ☐ How To _____
- ☐ Folklore _____
- ☐ Travel _____
- ☐ Other _____

Fiction

- ☐ Mystery _____
- ☐ Adventure _____
- ☐ Fantasy _____
- ☐ Realistic Fiction _____
- ☐ Historical Fiction _____
- ☐ Science Fiction _____
- ☐ Humor _____
- ☐ Animal Stories _____
- ☐ Other _____

LAURA'S Tips

When students have trouble finding a book, examine their Reading Interest Survey and Book Genre Questionnaire to help you identify new books they might enjoy. The Activities and Interests chart on page 130 is also helpful when determining student interests.

• • • • • • • • •

BOOK GENRE QUESTIONNAIRE

Name _____ Date _____

Which of the following types of books do you like? For each type of book that you like, try to think of an example or a specific topic. This will assist me in helping you find more great books!

Nonfiction   Examples of Topics or Books You Like

- ❑ Biographies _____

- ❑ Science _____

- ❑ History _____

- ❑ Poetry _____

- ❑ Supernatural _____

- ❑ How To _____

- ❑ Folklore _____

- ❑ Travel _____

- ❑ Other _____

Fiction

- ❑ Mystery _____

- ❑ Adventure _____

- ❑ Fantasy _____

- ❑ Realistic Fiction _____

- ❑ Historical Fiction _____

- ❑ Science Fiction _____

- ❑ Humor _____

- ❑ Animal Stories _____

- ❑ Other _____

CHAPTER 4

Power Reading Tools

Power Reading Tools

• • • • • • • • • •

Reading Workshop will have a powerful impact on your classroom. As your students learn to select books they enjoy and develop the stamina to read for long periods of time, you'll notice a subtle change in the energy level in your classroom. Reading will become a treasured time in the day, and your classroom will become a calm oasis of contented readers.

A quiet classroom of happy readers is nice, but will these methods actually boost reading achievement? The basic Reading Workshop alone might not be enough to transform poor readers into proficient ones. Without adding strategies to motivate and challenge your students, they might learn to love reading, but not actually become better readers.

How is that possible?

Undoubtedly, there are many reasons for this discrepancy, but some may relate to school requirements or student choice. What we require them to read at school, and even what they choose to read on their own, might not help them become better readers.

Fiction versus Nonfiction

Historically, schools have required students to read massive amounts of fiction, yet we've given little attention to nonfiction. Many kids choose fiction when given the choice. Without guidance from a teacher, most kids head straight to the fiction section of the library. If students do pick up a nonfiction book, they often browse the pages and look at pictures instead of reading and connecting with the ideas presented in the text.

However, most reading tests are heavily weighted with nonfiction selections. Informational articles, biographies, recipes, how-to articles, and poems make up the largest percentage of reading tests, with a few stories sprinkled in for good measure.

Why are tests designed this way?

One reason might be that most of what we read is nonfiction. Living in the information age requires reading and sifting through massive amounts of information on a daily basis, from learning new skills to searching the Internet for information. Today's reading tests measure functional literacy. Presumably, the results will provide the diagnostic data we need to prepare our students for reading later in life.

Power Up Your Reading Workshop

Understanding the importance of nonfiction reading is a step in the right direction, but in order to excel, your students must also accept responsibility for their own development as readers. Using the Power Reading Tools in this section, you will guide your students to gain more from all of their reading. They will explore a variety of genres, set personal reading goals, respond to literature in meaningful ways, and reflect on their own learning.

These twelve Power Reading Tools will power up your basic Reading Workshop and take it to the next level. Each Power Reading Tool includes directions for how to implement it in your Reading Workshop, as well as any reproducible forms needed for the lesson.

When to Add the Power Reading Tools

You'll have to decide when the time is right to begin adding each Power Reading Tool to your Reading Workshop. Be sure you and your students are comfortable with the basic Reading Workshop format before you start adding the tools. Age and maturity are important factors. Younger students may not be ready for some aspects of a more advanced Reading Workshop, so you'll need to select the components that meet your students' needs.

These lessons should be integrated into the normal flow of your basic Reading Workshop. When you introduce each new Power Reading Tool, you can use the suggested strategies in place of your regular mini-lesson for that day. In order to preserve the daily time for independent reading and conferring, you may need to stretch the Power Reading Tool instruction out over several days, perhaps introducing just one new tool each week.

From Reading Teacher to Reading Coach

As you implement the Power Reading Tools and students accept more responsibility for becoming better readers, reading instruction in your classroom will become student-centered rather than teacher-centered. You'll become a reading coach instead of a reading teacher. In so doing, you'll empower your students to love reading and to grow as readers.

POWER READING TOOLS

The Power Reading Tools are listed in the order that many teachers like to introduce them in the classroom. However, feel free to review the strategies and implement them in any order you feel is appropriate.

1 Power Reading Logs (Page 77)
Help students get organized by setting up an individual Power Reading Log. Each student will use this folder to store graphic organizers, goal forms, and other items related to Reading Workshop.

2 Everyday Reading:Fiction or Nonfiction?(Page 78)
Explore the different types of reading we do in everyday life to raise awareness about the difference between reading for pleasure and reading for life. Students will discover that about ninety percent of the reading we actually do in our everyday lives is nonfiction.

3 Flexible Guided Reading Groups (Page 81)
Meet with small groups of students during the independent reading time. Groups can be formed according to reading level or reading interest. They can also be formed to work with selected students on specific reading skills and strategies.

4 Book Challenges (Page 84)
Challenge your students to read a specific number of books across a variety of genres. Establish the challenge and use the record-keeping procedures needed to track their progress toward their goals.

5 Personal Goal Setting (Page 93)
Encourage students to set their own meaningful reading goals. Teach them how to set weekly reading goals and evaluate their progress.

6 Extended Written Response (Page 96)
Introduce journaling and letter writing as more complex forms of written response, which will help students deepen their understanding of texts.

▲7 Audio Books (Page 102)

Show students how they can improve both fluency and comprehension by listening to audio books as they follow along with the printed text.

▲8 Book Buzz (Page 105)

Students love to talk about what they are reading. Book Buzzes allow them to get together in small discussion groups to discuss their current books.

▲9 Magazine Power Hour (Page 109)

Magazines are fun to read and provide opportunities for students to read nonfiction. Add a Magazine Power Hour to your Reading Workshop once a month to supercharge it!

▲10 Graphic Organizers (Page 113)

Graphic organizers include both flat and folded methods for organizing and mapping information. Introduce graphic organizers to students and use a sample lesson based on *Jack and the Beanstalk* to help them understand the value of graphic organizers.

▲11 Self Assessment (Page 120)

Help students take responsibility for their growth as readers by encouraging them to reflect on their progress. You'll find specific strategies and rubrics for students to assess their own progress.

▲12 Strategic Planning (Page 124)

This tool is for you, rather than your students. Now that you've learned a variety of Power Reading Tools and strategies, you will need to create and write your own lesson plans. A planning form will help you organize future Reading Workshop lessons.

POWER READING TOOL 1 — Power Reading Logs

Materials

- 1 pocket folder for each student
- Students' completed forms:
  - My Reading Record forms
  - Reading Interest Surveys
  - Book Genre Questionnaires

Before you can introduce the Power Reading Tools, each student needs to set up a Power Reading Log to keep track of forms and records. Since this may take ten or fifteen minutes, you may not be able to teach your regular mini-lesson today. Be sure to allow time for independent reading, conferring with students, and closure.

Setting Up Power Reading Logs

By now each student should have a pocket folder, preferably plastic, that will be used to create their own Power Reading Log. Explain that now that they have settled in to the Reading Workshop routine, they are going to learn some additional strategies to become better readers. Setting up a Power Reading Log is the first step.

> **Have students place the following into their folders:**
> - My Reading Record forms (page 48)
> - Reading Interest Survey (page 42)
> - Book Genre Questionnaire (page 69)

It's helpful to invest in a three-hole punch device so that students can easily punch holes in their forms and fasten them into the folder. You can also have them add about ten sheets of lined paper at the back for notes and other forms of written response. You may also want them to include a blank copy of the Reading Wish List (page 92).

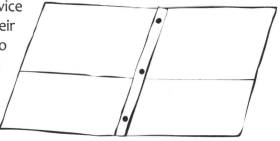

Using Power Reading Logs

As you introduce more organizers and record-keeping forms, have students add those forms to their logs. They can store their weekly Book Notes form in the front pocket of the folder. From now on, when you confer with students, ask them to bring their Power Reading Logs with them. You'll learn a great deal from each student's Log about what they are reading and how they are progressing toward their goals.

POWER READING TOOL 2: Everyday Reading: Fiction or Nonfiction?

Now that your students have set up their Power Reading Logs, it's time to introduce them to the importance of nonfiction reading in our everyday lives. These activities should be completed in the suggested order, but it may take you more than one day to complete all three.

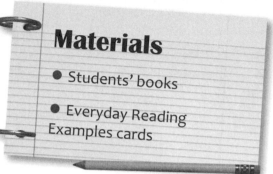

Materials

- Students' books

- Everyday Reading Examples cards

Activity 1:
What Are We Reading Now?

1 Ask students to take out what they are currently reading and consult with a partner about whether it is fiction or nonfiction.

2 Designate two different areas of the room, one for fiction and one for nonfiction. Ask students to move to one area depending on whether their current reading material is fiction or nonfiction.

3 Count the number in each group and display the result as a fraction or percentage. If your classroom is like most, the fiction side will far outnumber the nonfiction side.

Activity 2:
What Do We Read in Everyday Life?

1 After students return to their seats, ask them what kinds of reading they think most people do in everyday life. Ask everyone to jot down at least three types of reading they do outside of school.

2 If they have trouble thinking of everyday examples, give them a few ideas to get started. Mention examples similar to the ones on the Everyday Reading Examples cards, but don't actually show the cards yet.

3 Do a quick "popcorn share" by having each student, in turn, pop up and state one type of reading. Ask them to say whether each example is fiction or nonfiction. Some will share examples of fiction, but as they begin to think more deeply they will realize that most of what they read is actually nonfiction.

Activity 3:
Sorting Everyday Reading Examples Cards

1 Group your students in teams of three or four.

2 Give each team a set of the Everyday Reading Examples cards and have them place the cards face down in a pile in the middle.

3 Each team member takes turns flipping over a card and classifying it as fiction or nonfiction. Team members must discuss and agree on the classification of each card.

4 After all the cards are classified, discuss the fact that about ninety percent of what people read every day is nonfiction. (*Mystery novel* is the only fiction example in the set of cards.)

EVERYDAY READING EXAMPLES	
Ingredients and directions in a recipe	Directions for assembling a product (i.e. bike, bookcase, etc.)
Biography of a celebrity	Mystery novel
Internet search results	Nutrition information on a food package
Headline story in a local newspaper	Terms of agreement for software or websites
Travel guides and information	Magazine article about how to be a good friend

Extension Activity: Home Interviews

Ask students to interview at least one adult at home to find out what types of reading that person has done that day. Allow your students to share their results at your next Reading Workshop.

Everyday Reading Examples

Ingredients and directions in a recipe	Directions for assembling a product (i.e. bike, bookcase, etc.)
Biography of a celebrity	Mystery novel
Internet search results	Nutrition information on a food package
Headline story in a local newspaper	Terms of agreement for software or websites
Travel guides and information	Magazine article about how to be a good friend

POWER READING TOOL 3 — Flexible Guided Reading Groups

You've been conferring individually with your students during the basic Reading Workshop, but those conferences can be very time intensive. In addition, individual conferences may not provide adequate support for struggling readers. Flexible Guided Reading Groups add another way for you to add reading instruction to your Reading Workshop. It's best to seek a balance between individual and group work.

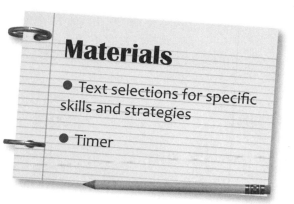

Materials
- Text selections for specific skills and strategies
- Timer

Creating Flexible Guided Reading Groups

The word "flexible" is the key to making guided reading groups work. Students who are permanently placed in a low reading group will never learn to love reading. They'll be humiliated by the experience, and no amount of instruction will ever overcome their mindset for failure.

Create new groups at least every week, and make sure that all students are included, even if you only meet with some groups once during the week. Let students know that you are creating groups to work on specific skills or with specific types of texts, and that you look forward to having more time to interact with them and learn about them as readers.

Keep group sizes as small as possible. Five or six students in a group are plenty. If you have more than that, you won't have time to interact with them effectively. Each week, or whenever you change groups, post a master list with the names of the students in each group. To make it easy to refer to the groups, label the groups with a letter, such as "Group A," or a silly name, such as "Rockin' Readers." But don't make the "A" group be the best readers every week. Mix it up, and sometimes create the groups randomly.

When and How to Meet with Guided Reading Groups

Flexible Guided Reading Groups take place during your independent reading time.

- Start by meeting with just one group per day for twenty minutes or so, working to improve transitions and management before attempting to meet with several groups a day. Conducting these sessions without disturbing the rest of the class can be tricky. Since the other students will be reading silently, your students who are coming to the small group will need to move to the meeting area quickly and quietly. Sit close together around a table or on the floor and whisper as you talk. It helps if students know in advance which group will be meeting and what they are expected to bring with them.

● It's not necessary to meet with all students every day. Many teachers meet with their struggling readers every day and meet with the other students only once or twice a week. Flexibility is the key. Finding the right amount of time to meet with each group may take some experimentation.

● Despite your best intentions, some students who are not in the group will have trouble concentrating while the group is meeting. You need to preserve at least twenty minutes of the reading block as a time when everyone is reading silently and no one is meeting in a group. Your goal is not to see how many group meetings you can squeeze into a day or even a week, but to support students within the framework of the Reading Workshop.

What to Do in Guided Reading Groups

Guided reading is not round robin reading. In these sessions, you will work with small groups of students on what they most need in order to grow as readers. All students can benefit from small group instruction, whether they are proficient or struggling readers.

Use short texts, such as leveled readers or magazine articles, to introduce and model specific skills or strategies. Differentiate your instruction by adjusting the reading level or type of text according to the needs of each group.

To begin the lesson, preview the text with them, and then ask them to read portions of the text independently. As they finish each section, discuss how they were able to apply the strategy to the given text. Here are a few ideas to get you started working with flexible guided reading groups:

- Identifying nonfiction text features and structure
- Using a new graphic organizer
- Using context clues to figure out the meaning of unknown words
- Applying specific comprehension strategies such as inference and prediction
- Analyzing character traits and motives
- Identifying story elements such as setting, plot, and theme
- Determining the author's purpose in writing the text

Resources

Loads of books and resources are available about how to implement guided reading groups. The best resource I have found is *Guided Reading Groups in Grades 3-6* by Mary Browning Shulman. Besides giving step-by-step directions, she provides 20 one-page reading passages, mostly on nonfiction topics, that are perfect for guided reading groups. You can find more information about guided reading instruction in the Appendix.

LAURA'S Tips

Don't try to conduct individual conferences and guided reading groups on the same day or even during the same week. I like to alternate weeks so that one week I'm meeting with my students individually and then next I conduct small group instruction.

● ● ● ● ● ● ● ● ●

POWER READING TOOL 4 Book Challenges

After discussing the discrepancy between school reading and everyday reading, it's time to engage your students in strategies to close that gap. Issuing a Book Challenge is a great way to begin. The 40-Book Challenge is designed for older students or stronger readers who need to increase the variety of their reading materials. The 20-Book Challenge is a variation that works for younger students or struggling readers, encouraging them to read longer books without regard to genre.

Materials

- Power Reading Logs
- Book Challenge forms

40-Book Challenge

The Book Challenge strategy comes from *The Book Whisperer*, a must-read for anyone implementing a Reading Workshop. The author, Donalyn Miller, challenges her students to read at least forty books during the school year, and she provides a list of genres to encourage variety in their reading. Students are not graded on their progress or penalized for not reading forty books; they are simply challenged to meet this goal. I adapted her idea by creating a chart that provides us with a useful visual record. Students must read books in a variety of genres in order to complete the entire chart, and it's easy to see at a glance which categories they have completed.

☽ THE 40-BOOK CHALLENGE							
Informational	Informational	Realistic Fiction	Mystery	Mystery	My Choice	My Choice	My Choice
Informational	Informational	Realistic Fiction	Fantasy	Fantasy	My Choice	My Choice	My Choice
Informational	Informational	Historical Fiction	Folklore	Folklore	My Choice	My Choice	My Choice
Informational	Informational	Historical Fiction	Poetry	Poetry	My Choice	My Choice	My Choice
Informational	Informational	Science Fiction	Biography	Biography	My Choice	My Choice	My Choice

Two variations of the 40-Book Challenge chart are found on pages 87 and 88. Choose the chart that best meets your needs. The one with the moon icon is more open-ended and allows for more choice. The one with the star is more specific. If you want to create your own version, use the blank chart on page 89.

What to Do:

- Introduce the Book Challenge to your students by reminding them that most people tend to read a lot of fiction, but adults read a much greater variety of genres in everyday life. Tell them that you want to challenge them to read many different types of books during the year. They may even find a new favorite genre!

- Distribute one copy of your selected 40-Book Challenge chart to each student. Ask them to place the chart as the first page inside their Power Reading Log. As your students finish reading each book, they will record the book's title in the appropriate block.

- Review your students' Book Challenge forms on a regular basis. After a few weeks, you'll notice patterns in your students' reading preferences. When you confer with them, you will want to discuss their progress toward their 40-Book Challenge. Many of your students will notice the fiction or nonfiction gaps on their chart, and it will motivate them to seek out other types of reading materials.

LAURA'S Tips

My students realized that in order to meet the 40-Book Challenge in one school year, they needed to read at least ten books per quarter. We counted books of three hundred pages or more as two books and recorded their titles in two different blocks. We also found it helpful to color-code the blocks after they added a title. They put blue dots next to titles they read during the first quarter, red dots next to titles for the second quarter, and so on. By doing so, we were able to track their performance from one quarter to the next.

20-Book Challenge

Reading forty books may be unrealistic for some students. If so, you can issue a 20-Book Challenge. The 20-Book Challenge chart is not organized by genres; instead, it's organized to encourage kids to read longer books. Many children reach a stage in their reading progress where they are able to read longer books, but don't do so, because they are intimidated by the length of the book.

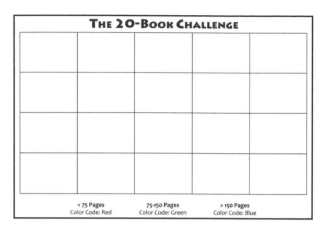

To use this chart, have students record each title in a separate block after they finish reading each book. Then ask them to color-code each block by shading it lightly according to the length of the book. Red denotes books of less than 75 pages, green shows books that are 75 to 150 pages in length, and blue indicates books that are longer than 150 pages. Be sure to compliment students on the number of green and blue boxes because those colors indicate that your students are reading longer books.

LAURA'S Tips

It's exciting that many students will want to complete more than one Book Challenge chart! But be on the lookout for students who rush through their books just to record them on the chart. If this starts to happen, you might want to require that students have a conference with you about each book before they add it to their charts.

Note: You can download customizable Book Challenge forms from my website (www.lauracandler.com/prw).

THE 40-BOOK CHALLENGE

Informational	Informational	Informational	Informational	Informational
Informational	Informational	Informational	Informational	Informational
Realistic Fiction	Realistic Fiction	Historical Fiction	Historical Fiction	Science Fiction
Mystery	Fantasy	Folklore	Poetry	Biography
Mystery	Fantasy	Folklore	Poetry	Biography
My Choice	My Choice	My Choice	My Choice	My Choice
My Choice	My Choice	My Choice	My Choice	My Choice
My Choice	My Choice	My Choice	My Choice	My Choice

The 40-Book Challenge

Realistic Fiction	Historical Fiction	Fantasy	Informational	Mystery	Chapter Book Choice	Chapter Book Choice
Realistic Fiction	Historical Fiction	Fantasy	Informational	Science Fiction	Science Fiction	Chapter Book Choice
Realistic Fiction	Historical Fiction	Fantasy	Informational	Folklore	Folklore	Chapter Book Choice
Realistic Fiction	Historical Fiction	Fantasy	Informational	Poetry	Poetry	Chapter Book Choice
Realistic Fiction	Historical Fiction	Fantasy	Informational	Biography	Biography	Chapter Book Choice

THE 40-BOOK CHALLENGE

THE 20-BOOK CHALLENGE

< 75 Pages
Color Code: Red

75-150 Pages
Color Code: Green

> 150 Pages
Color Code: Blue

OTHER BOOK CHALLENGE RESOURCES

Certificates of Achievement

Many teachers feel that students deserve some type of reward for completing a Book Challenge. Others worry that offering something tangible will have long-term negative consequences, as students become conditioned to read for external rewards. Hopefully, your students will feel a sense of accomplishment when they complete a Book Challenge, but if you want something more, you could present them with a Certificate of Achievement. You'll find three sample certificates on pages 132 to 134 that were designed to keep the focus on reading achievement. These certificates offer a simple congratulations along with the words, "Celebrate the joy of reading!"

Reading Wish Lists

The whole idea of a Book Challenge may be overwhelming to your students. It might help them to plan ahead by keeping a list of books they want to read in the future. You can have students record the titles on a sheet of paper or give them copies of the Reading Wish List on page 92. As students hear about a book they would like to read in the future, they record its title, author, and genre on the chart. Students keep this list in their Power Reading Logs, and they check off the titles as they read them.

You can facilitate the planning process by giving students regular opportunities to share their favorite books with their classmates. One easy way to do this is to start or end with a daily "One Minute Book Share," in which students talk about a favorite book from a particular genre. Ask students to sign up in advance to be sure they are prepared to share information about their books. At the end of each sharing session, students who are interested in that particular title can record the book on their Reading Wish Lists.

Laura's Tips

Without using a computerized tracking program such as Accelerated Reader, it can be difficult to determine if your students are actually reading their books. Despite this difficulty, I'm not in favor of requiring students to fill out a book report or project to "get credit" for reading. Monitor their reading progress by conferring with them on a regular basis and reviewing their reading records when you meet.

Reading Wish List

Title	Author	Genre	✓

POWER READING TOOL 5 Personal Goal Setting

After introducing a Book Challenge to your students, you can engage them in setting weekly reading goals. Book Challenges are long-term goals set by the teacher, but weekly goals are short personal goals that students set for themselves as they begin to take responsibility for their own learning. Since this lesson works best on Monday, feel free to skip it and return to it later.

Materials

- Power Reading Logs
- My Weekly Reading Goals forms
- Goal-setting example

Create Your Own Goal

Before you begin this lesson, take a few moments to create your own weekly reading goal and be prepared to use yourself as an example during the lesson. Personal goals should be short and focused, and they should be something that can be completed in a week. Consider the following possible reading goals:

- Read a nonfiction book
- Finish 50 pages of the book I'm currently reading
- Start reading a book by _____ (author)
- Start a book from a particular genre (biography, science fiction, historical fiction, folklore, etc.)
- Read a magazine or newspaper article
- Start reading a challenging book
- Find a really good book on _____ (topic)
- Write more thoughtful reading responses each day
- Remember to stop and reread when I don't understand the story

Introduce the Lesson

To begin the lesson, explain to your students that while completing the Book Challenge is a worthy goal, they need smaller goals along the way to keep them motivated. Point out that the Book Challenge is not a personal goal because it's a challenge you have issued to them. Now you would like them to set personal goals for what they want to accomplish themselves.

Distribute the My Weekly Reading Goals form and discuss the characteristics of a personal goal. According to Dr. Steven Layne in *Igniting a Passion for Reading*, a strong goal will stretch you and motivate you, but it will also be reasonable. While your students watch, fill out the top section of the goal-setting form by writing a simple weekly goal for yourself. Tell them that at the end of the week you will review your goal and decide whether or not you achieved it.

Brainstorm and Write Weekly Goals

Ask your students to share their ideas for weekly goals. Write their goal suggestions on chart paper to keep for future reference. If your students can't think of any weekly goals, prompt them by suggesting some of the ideas above. Then give your students a few minutes to complete the top sections of their own forms. If you have started your flexible guided reading groups, you can teach one small group at a time how to write simple yet effective goal statements. Have your students store the My Weekly Reading Goals forms in their Power Reading Logs.

Evaluate Progress

At the end of the week, take out your own form and show it to your students. Tell your students whether or not you achieved your goal. Then circle *yes* or *no* and model how to write a brief comment. A comment could explain why you didn't make the goal or perhaps how you exceeded your goal. For example, if you planned to read fifty pages and you read seventy-five, you could make a note of that in the comment area. Then ask your students to take out their forms and complete the evaluation section. Right after they complete that section, they may write a new goal for the coming week, or they may wait until Monday to write a new goal.

Personal Goal Conferences

Throughout the next week, meet with several students each day to discuss and review their goals. Be sure to check in with every student before the end of the week. Remind students to store their goal forms in their Power Reading Logs and keep them from week to week so you can observe their progress over time. Encourage them to set different goals each week, and to write goals that will help them improve their reading skills.

If you don't want to duplicate the My Weekly Reading Goals form, you can have students record their goals on the backs of their weekly Book Notes forms. Be sure to have them review their goals at the end of the week and write whether or not they were accomplished.

Name _____

MY WEEKLY READING GOALS

Week of _____

My reading goal for this week is _____

_____

Achieved? ❑ Yes   ❑ No   Comment _____

• • • • • • • • •

Week of _____

My reading goal for this week is _____

_____

Achieved? ❑ Yes   ❑ No   Comment _____

• • • • • • • • •

Week of _____

My reading goal for this week is _____

_____

Achieved? ❑ Yes   ❑ No   Comment _____

• • • • • • • • •

Week of _____

My reading goal for this week is _____

_____

Achieved? ❑ Yes   ❑ No   Comment _____

POWER READING TOOL 6 — Extended Written Response

For the first few weeks, using the Book Notes form is sufficient to keep you in touch with what your students are reading. But now that your students enjoy reading and are becoming more thoughtful readers, it's time to introduce them to longer forms of written response: Power Reading Journals and Reading Letters. Stagger their use so students aren't doing both in the same week.

Materials

- Journal Prompts and lined sheets
- Previously-read book
- Reading Is Thinking chart from Day 5
- Reading Letter Prompts

A. Power Reading Journals

An easy way to make the transition to more thoughtful written response to reading is to introduce Power Reading Journals for each student.

You can create a simple 5½" x 8½" journal by reproducing the forms that follow or by downloading the forms from my website (www.lauracandler.com/prw).

My Power Reading Journal

by Tina Lee

- Duplicate the Journal Prompts page on 8½"x 11" card stock or construction paper and fold each sheet in half with the prompts on the inside.

- Duplicate three or four lined journal pages for each student.

- Fold the lined sheets, tuck them inside the covers, and staple along each spine.

- Have students add their name and a title to the cover of their journal.

Students like these journals because the small size makes them less intimidating than a sheet of notebook paper. Depending on whether they are reading fiction or nonfiction, they can use the appropriate journal response prompts found on the inside of the cover. Once or twice a week, you can assign a prompt or allow students to select one on their own. Since these prompts require more writing than the Book Notes, you'll need to allow more class time for responding after reading. If they don't finish in class, allow your students to take their journals with them to complete at home.

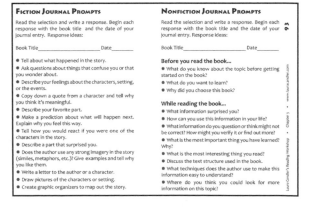

FICTION JOURNAL PROMPTS

Read the selection and write a response. Begin each response with the book title and the date of your journal entry. Response ideas:

Book Title_____ Date_____

- Tell about what happened in the story.
- Ask questions about things that confuse you or that you wonder about.
- Describe your feelings about the characters, setting, or the events.
- Copy down a quote from a character and tell why you think it's meaningful.
- Describe your favorite part.
- Make a prediction about what will happen next. Explain why you feel this way.
- Tell how you would react if you were one of the characters in the story.
- Describe a part that surprised you.
- Does the author use any strong imagery in the story (similes, metaphors, etc.)? Give examples and tell why you like them.
- Write a letter to the author or a character.
- Draw pictures of the characters or setting.
- Create graphic organizers to map out the story.

NONFICTION JOURNAL PROMPTS

Read the selection and write a response. Begin each response with the book title and the date of your journal entry. Response ideas:

Book Title_____ Date_____

Before you read the book...
- What do you know about the topic before getting started on the book?
- What do you want to learn?
- Why did you choose this book?

While reading the book...
- What information surprised you?
- How can you use this information in your life?
- What information do you question or think might not be correct? How might you verify it or find out more?
- What is the most important thing you have learned? Why?
- What is the most interesting thing you read?
- Discuss the text structure used in the book.
- What techniques does the author use to make this information easy to understand?
- Where do you think you could look for more information on this topic?

Fiction Journal Prompts

Read the selection and write a response. Begin each response with the book title and the date of your journal entry. Response ideas:

Book Title _____   Date _____

- Tell about what happened in the story.
- Ask questions about things that confuse you or that you wonder about.
- Describe your feelings about the characters, setting, or the events.
- Copy down a quote from a character and tell why you think it's meaningful.
- Describe your favorite part.
- Make a prediction about what will happen next. Explain why you feel this way.
- Tell how you would react if you were one of the characters in the story.
- Describe a part that surprised you.
- Does the author use any strong imagery in the story (similes, metaphors, etc.)? Give examples and tell why you like them.
- Write a letter to the author or a character.
- Draw pictures of the characters or setting.
- Create graphic organizers to map out the story.

Nonfiction Journal Prompts

Read the selection and write a response. Begin each response with the book title and the date of your journal entry. Response ideas:

Book Title _____   Date _____

Before you read the book...

- What do you know about the topic before getting started on the book?
- What do you want to learn?
- Why did you choose this book?

While reading the book...

- What information surprised you?
- How can you use this information in your life?
- What information do you question or think might not be correct? How might you verify it or find out more?
- What is the most important thing you have learned? Why?
- What is the most interesting thing you read?
- Discuss the text structure used in the book.
- What techniques does the author use to make this information easy to understand?
- Where do you think you could look for more information on this topic?

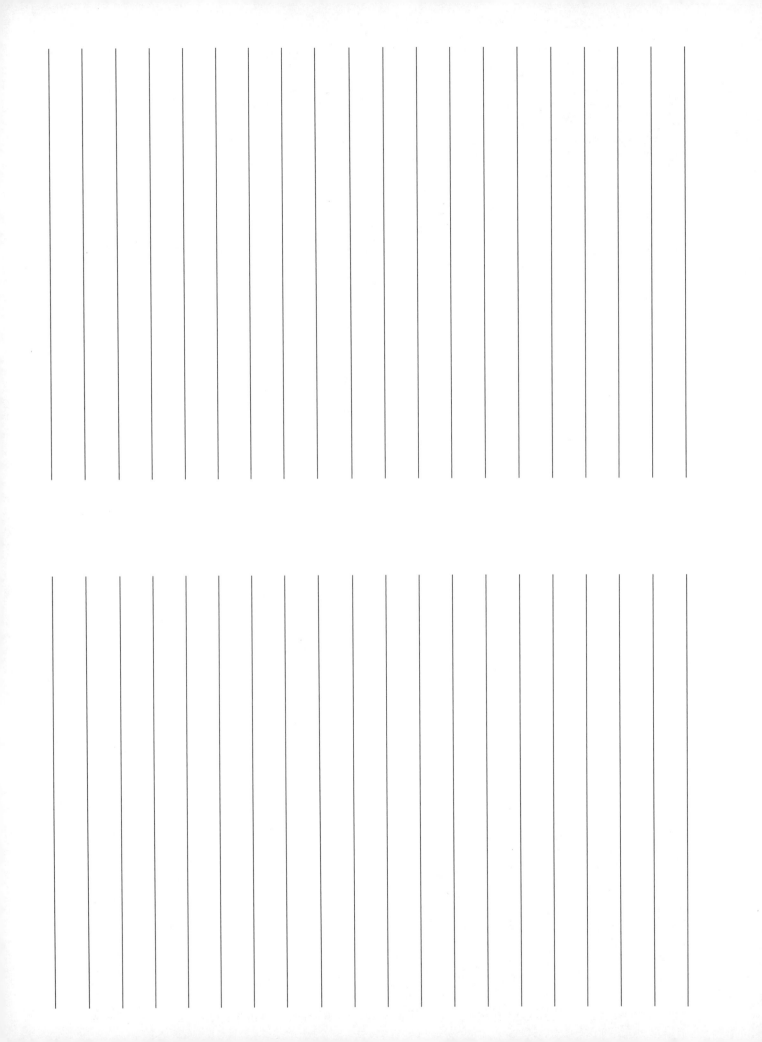

B. Reading Letters

Another way to extend students' written responses to what they are reading is through the use of the Reading Letters tool. Once a week, ask your students to write a Reading Letter to you, telling you about what they are reading and what they are thinking about as they read. On that day, skip your mini-lesson to allow time for students to write you a Reading Letter.

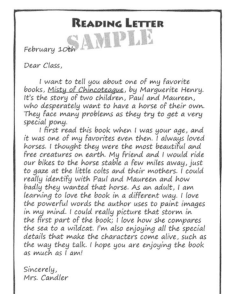

READING LETTER

SAMPLE

February 10th

Dear Class,

I want to tell you about one of my favorite books, Misty of Chincoteague, by Marguerite Henry. It's the story of two children, Paul and Maureen, who desperately want to have a horse of their own. They face many problems as they try to get a very special pony.

I first read this book when I was your age, and it was one of my favorites even then. I always loved horses. I thought they were the most beautiful and free creatures on earth. My friend and I would ride our bikes to the horse stable a few miles away, just to gaze at the little colts and their mothers. I could really identify with Paul and Maureen and how badly they wanted that horse. As an adult, I am learning to love the book in a different way. I love the powerful words the author uses to paint images in my mind. I could really picture that storm in the first part of the book; I love how she compares the sea to a wildcat. I'm also enjoying all the special details that make the characters come alive, such as the way they talk. I hope you are enjoying the book as much as I am!

Sincerely,
Mrs. Candler

What to Do:

1 To introduce Reading Letters, tell your students that you are interested in what they are reading and, more importantly, what they are thinking about their reading. Refer back to the Reading Is Thinking list you created Day 5. What kinds of strategies are they using as they read?

2 Reading Letters should be two paragraphs long: the first paragraph briefly summarizes what they have read, and the second paragraph tells you about what they are thinking about what they have read. Students can write their Reading Letters in their Power Reading Journals or on loose-leaf notebook paper.

3 Model how to write a Reading Letter, using a book you have previously read to the class. Show them how to write a brief summary, followed by a paragraph that focuses on their thinking. The Sample Reading Letter on page 101 is a guide you can use to compose your model Reading Letter.

4 Post the Reading Letter Prompts (page 100) or give each student a copy to keep in his or her Power Reading Log. Remind them to look at the list if they get stuck and can't think of anything to write.

5 Allow at least twenty minutes of class time for this activity, rather than assigning it for homework. Your students will write more thoughtful responses if they have time to compose their letters in class.

Teacher Response to Journals and Reading Letters

After your students write in their journals or write reading letters, it's important that you read them and respond in some way. You don't have to take home a stack of journals or letters to grade; you can read them quickly prior to conferring with each student. You can respond by writing directly on each journal page, or you can talk with your students about their entries and letters when you confer with them. As you read and respond to what they've written, you'll gather a wealth of information about your students and their reading progress.

Reading Letter Prompts

This year we will write letters to each other about books and what we are reading. When you write your Reading Letters, start with a short paragraph that summarizes what you have been reading. Then write another paragraph in which you share your thinking about the book. For example, you might:

- Tell what you like/dislike about a book and why you feel that way.

- Tell about what puzzled you or made you ask questions.

- Tell what you noticed about the characters, such as what made them act the way they did or how they changed.

- Write about something in the book that surprised you.

- Write your predictions, and later tell whether you were right.

- Ask for help to understand a passage or part of the book.

- Tell about the connections that you made while reading the book. Tell how it reminds you of yourself, of people you know, or of something that happened in your life. It might even remind you of other books, especially the characters, the events, or the setting.

- Write about the author's style and how it makes you feel.

- Write about the language the author used and why you think the author chose this style of writing or chose to use certain images.

I look forward to reading your letters!

READING LETTER

SAMPLE

February 10th

Dear Class,

I want to tell you about one of my favorite books, <u>Misty of Chincoteague</u>, by Marguerite Henry. It's the story of two children, Paul and Maureen, who desperately want to have a horse of their own. They face many problems as they try to get a very special pony.

I first read this book when I was your age, and it was one of my favorites even then. I always loved horses. I thought they were the most beautiful and free creatures on earth. My friend and I would ride our bikes to the horse stable a few miles away, just to gaze at the little colts and their mothers. I could really identify with Paul and Maureen and how badly they wanted that horse. As an adult, I am learning to love the book in a different way. I love the powerful words the author uses to paint images in my mind. I could really picture that storm in the first part of the book; I love how she compares the sea to a wildcat. I'm also enjoying all the special details that make the characters come alive, such as the way they talk. I hope you are enjoying the book as much as I am!

Sincerely,
Mrs. Candler

Audio books can be powerful additions to any reading classroom. When students listen as they read along in a book, they improve both fluency and comprehension.

Several years ago I conducted an action research study to test how audio books improve reading skills. I selected eight struggling readers for my study, and I provided audio materials for every book that they read over a two-month period. I compared their quarterly test scores before and after the study, and every single student made significant gains. The average score rose from 41% correct in September to 60% correct in December!

Why do audio books have such an impact? How do improved listening skills translate to improved reading skills?

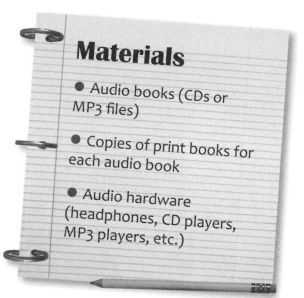

Materials

- Audio books (CDs or MP3 files)
- Copies of print books for each audio book
- Audio hardware (headphones, CD players, MP3 players, etc.)

The Power of Audio Books

I believe that audio books can introduce students to a world of reading they've never known. Fifth graders who can't read well probably aren't motivated by a steady diet of *Junie B. Jones* and *Horrible Harry* books. But hook them up to an audio version of *Hatchet*, and the words begin to work their magic. As your students track the text with their eyes and listen with their ears, they see words they've heard before but were not able to recognize in print. They can apply the strategies that good readers use, from visualizing the events to making predictions. In the process, they discover the joys of a great book!

Many teachers worry that students will use audio books as a crutch and never

learn to read well on their own. Surprisingly, that's not what generally happens. In my experience, as students become better readers, they naturally relinquish the audio support. Why get out a CD player and search for the right track when you can read the book without it?

Preferred Formats for Audio Materials

CDs and MP3 files are best for today's classrooms. Cassette tapes are outdated and have to be rewound constantly. CD players are inexpensive, and you can buy headphone splitters, which are adapters that allow more than one set of headphones to be plugged into a player. By stacking these adapters, you can have as many as four or five students connected to one player.

Using Audio Books in Reading Workshop

All students enjoy listening to audio books from time to time, but your struggling readers will benefit the most from regular access to audio materials. Gather your available audio books and listening hardware, and then identify a few students who will begin using them. Audio books should be recorded on the Reading Record form in the same way as any other book. Teach your students how to use the hardware to fast forward and rewind to the correct location, and make sure they know that they must follow along in their books as they listen. To prevent them from getting drowsy while listening, it's best if they sit at a desk with both the audio player and the book in front of them. Remind students to store the materials properly when they finish. If you allow students to check out the CD for home listening, you may want to create a back-up copy first.

LAURA's Tips

I store all audio materials in the drawers of a plastic rolling cart. Create a set of classroom audio CDs from the original CDs and keep the originals in a safe place. That way if a CD is lost, damaged, or stolen, you can easily create a replacement. Store one copy of the book in a plastic zip bag with the set of CDs. One of our classroom jobs is Audio Materials Manager, and that person is responsible for making sure the books, CDs, headphones, and CD players are stored properly. Allow students who have demonstrated that they are reliable and trustworthy to check out CDs to take home.

Obtaining Audio Collections and Hardware

Here are some ideas to help you find and fund audio books and equipment for your Reading Workshop:

- Check with your school's media coordinator to see what audio materials are available on site.
- Send a letter to parents asking for donations that you can use to purchase materials for your program.
- Search for audio books at your local public library.
- Find out about community-funded educational grants.
- Ask local businesses to donate money to purchase hardware and CDs.
- Scout for audio books, paperback books, and hardware at yard sales.
- Ask your school's PTA for money to support your program.

LAURA'S Tips

Be sure to check out DonorsChoose.org, an organization that matches donors with classrooms and provides funding for educational projects. I've personally obtained over $1,500 worth of materials from DonorsChoose.org, and I know many other teachers who have had similar success.

● ● ● ● ● ● ● ● ●

Book Buzz is based on a discussion strategy in Steven Layne's *Igniting a Passion for Reading*. In a Book Buzz, unlike other book discussion groups, everyone is reading something different. To give the group a focal point for meaningful discussion, Layne suggests having the students rate their books and respond to a question prior to meeting with their group.

Materials

- Book Buzz Notes
- Book Buzz Focus Questions
- Timer

What to Do:

1 TEACHER PREPARATION – Divide your class into semi-permanent teams of three to five students. You want some variety in each group, but you also want students to feel comfortable with their Book Buzz buddies. These groups will meet once or twice a week and will stay together for several months at a time. Duplicate one copy of the Book Buzz Notes on page 107 for each student.

2 INDEPENDENT READING – On the day you plan to introduce the Book Buzz strategy, skip your usual mini-lesson and give students at least twenty to thirty minutes of independent reading time at the beginning of class. Then have them return to their seats to prepare for their meetings. Allow a total of at least thirty minutes for meeting preparation time and the Book Buzz discussions.

3 MEETING PREPARATION – After students return to their seats from reading, give them each a copy of the Book Buzz Notes form and post two questions from the Book Buzz Focus Questions, one for fiction and one for nonfiction (see examples on the bottom of page 108.) Students complete the top portion (title, author, page number, rating) and record whether their books are fiction or nonfiction. Then give them about five minutes to jot down the question and their responses.

4 STUDENTS CIRCLE UP – Assign each group a location in the room to circle up for their discussion. They can sit on the floor, move desks, or bring a chair to the location, but they should all be on the same level, looking at each other eye-to-eye.

5 BOOK BUZZ MEETINGS – Now the fun begins as students discuss their books and responses to the question! Each person begins by sharing the title, author, and their rating. Then they explain their response to the focus question. After they take turns sharing, the remaining time can be used for open discussion about all of their books. If you're concerned that team members are not participating equally, you may want to provide more structure. For example, you could set a timer and allow each person on the team two or three minutes for sharing.

6 REFLECTION – At the end of the activity, have students rate their participation on the day's Book Buzz Notes. You can also have them turn their papers over and write a reflection about the Book Buzz activity and how their group worked together.

Name _____ Date _____

BOOK BUZZ NOTES

Title _____

Rating so far: ☆ ☆ ☆ ☆ ☆   ☐ Fiction
                                   ☐ Nonfiction
Author _____   Page Number _____
Focus Question: _____
_____
_____

Response to Focus Question: _____
_____
_____
_____
_____
_____
_____
_____

My participation in the Book Buzz today was:

☐ Excellent   ☐ Good   ☐ Fair   ☐ Poor

Name _____ Date _____

BOOK BUZZ NOTES

Title _____

Rating so far: ☆ ☆ ☆ ☆ ☆   ❑ Fiction
                                ❑ Nonfiction

Author _____ Page Number _____

Focus Question: _____

_____

_____

_____

Response to Focus Question: _____

_____

_____

_____

_____

_____

_____

_____

_____

My participation in the Book Buzz today was:

❑ Excellent   ❑ Good   ❑ Fair   ❑ Poor

BOOK BUZZ FOCUS QUESTIONS

Fiction Question _____

_____

_____

_____

Nonfiction Question _____

_____

_____

_____

Suggested Book Buzz Questions

Fiction

- What is the problem in this book? How do you predict that it will be solved?

- What kind of connections can you make between characters and events in this book and your own life?

- What character is the most interesting? Describe the character and explain why you find him or her to be fascinating.

- If you could meet the characters in this book, would you be friends with any of them? Why or why not?

- Explain why you rated the book with the number of stars you gave it.

- Would you recommend this book to others? Why or why not?

Nonfiction

- Why did you choose this book? Did it prove to be a good choice? Explain.

- How does the information in this book compare to information you already know about this topic?

- What have you learned from this book that might impact your life?

- What is the most interesting thing you have learned from this book?

- Would you recommend this book to others? Why or why not?

Most students love to read magazines. Did you know that reading magazines might actually boost reading performance? Most passages on standardized reading tests are very similar to magazine articles. Unlike fiction novels, articles are short and focused on a particular topic. They introduce challenging vocabulary using topics that interest kids. Magazine Power Hour taps into this natural affinity for magazines. To complete this activity in one day, you'll need to skip your usual mini-lesson to provide plenty of time for buddies to read and chat about their magazines.

Materials

- Age-appropriate magazines
- Magazine Power Hour forms
- Magazine Power Hour letters

Where to Find Reading Material

Before attempting this activity, take stock of the resources available to you:

- If your students have subscriptions to kids' magazines, you can send home the Magazine Power Hour letter (page 112) and have them bring in their magazines for that day.

- See what your media center has available. You might be able to borrow a variety of recent and old issues to take back to your classroom.

- If you plan in advance, you might be able to obtain grants or funding for magazine subscriptions to be delivered to your classroom.

- In addition to magazines, you can use newspapers. Do you have *Kidsville News* (www.kidsvillenews.com) delivered in your area? How about *Scholastic News* or *Weekly Reader*? You can certainly include them in your Magazine Power Hour.

MAGAZINE POWER HOUR

Dear Parents,

Magazines are fun to read, but did you know that reading them also improves comprehension and fluency? Soon our class is going to hold a Magazine Power Hour reading session. On this day, your child is invited to bring in age-appropriate magazines* to read during class and to share with others. In addition, students will be allowed to check out magazines from the library. Examples include *Ranger Rick*, *National Geographic for Kids*, *Sports Illustrated for Kids*, *American Girl*, and so on. Students aren't required to bring a magazine from home, but I wanted you to be aware of this option. Thanks for your support! We are looking forward to our Magazine Power Hour!

Magazine Power Hour Date and Time_____

Name _____

Parent Signature _____

* Note: I will need to approve all magazines brought from home.

What to Do:

1 ANNOUNCE MAGAZINE BUDDIES – Pair your students with a Magazine Buddy before the activity and announce them when the session begins. They will keep the same buddy throughout the activity.

2 READ INDEPENDENTLY – Ask your students to move to their special reading spots to read for about ten to twelve minutes. They may want to stay close to their reading buddies, but they shouldn't be reading the same magazine or reading together.

3 SHARE AND DISCUSS – When it appears that most students have finished at least one article, ask students to meet with their buddies for about five minutes. Have them complete the first sections of their Magazine Power Hour forms with information about their own articles. Then ask them to share and discuss what they learned while reading. On a signal from you, students return to their reading spots and read a new article.

4 SWAP MAGAZINES – If you have enough magazines, allow students to choose a new magazine or swap with their partner after each chat session.

5 REPEAT STEPS – Have students repeat these steps two more times so that they read and discuss a total of three articles.

6 WRITE REFLECTIONS – Near the end of the hour, provide time for them to write a reflection at the bottom of the page about their favorite article.

LAURA'S Tips

Because it may be difficult to find enough magazines to do the activity every week, you may want to limit Magazine Power Hour to special occasions or once a month.

Name _____ Date _____

Magazine Power Hour

Magazine Buddy _____

Magazines and Article Titles

1 Magazine _____ Issue _____
   Article _____ pp. _____

2 Magazine _____ Issue _____
   Article _____ pp. _____

3 Magazine _____ Issue _____
   Article _____ pp. _____

Which article was your favorite? What did you learn or what did you enjoy about reading it? What do you still want to know?

_____

_____

_____

_____

_____

_____

_____

_____

Magazine Power Hour

Dear Parents,

     Magazines are fun to read, but did you know that reading them also improves comprehension and fluency? Soon our class is going to hold a Magazine Power Hour reading session. On this day, your child is invited to bring in age-appropriate magazines* to read during class and to share with others. In addition, students will be allowed to check out magazines from the library. Examples include *Ranger Rick, National Geographic for Kids, Sports Illustrated for Kids, American Girl,* and so on. Students aren't required to bring a magazine from home, but I wanted you to be aware of this option. Thanks for your support! We are looking forward to our Magazine Power Hour!

Magazine Power Hour Date and Time _____

Name _____

Parent Signature _____

     ◆ Note: I will need to approve all magazines brought from home.

- -

Magazine Power Hour

Dear Parents,

     Magazines are fun to read, but did you know that reading them also improves comprehension and fluency? Soon our class is going to hold a Magazine Power Hour reading session. On this day, your child is invited to bring in age-appropriate magazines* to read during class and to share with others. In addition, students will be allowed to check out magazines from the library. Examples include *Ranger Rick, National Geographic for Kids, Sports Illustrated for Kids, American Girl,* and so on. Students aren't required to bring a magazine from home, but I wanted you to be aware of this option. Thanks for your support! We are looking forward to our Magazine Power Hour!

Magazine Power Hour Date and Time _____

Name _____

Parent Signature _____

     ◆ Note: I will need to approve all magazines brought from home.

POWER READING TOOL 10 Graphic Organizers

What do graphic organizers, mind maps, and 3-D note-taking folders all have in common? These tools help us organize and conceptualize information so we can better understand it. Graphic organizers allow us to sort, classify, and manipulate new concepts, which results in higher retention of information and leads to new insights.

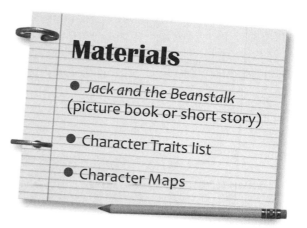

Materials

- *Jack and the Beanstalk* (picture book or short story)
- Character Traits list
- Character Maps

Even though many graphic organizers seem intuitive to adults, students need specific instruction in how to use them. Below you'll find a generic lesson plan that can be used with almost any graphic organizer, as well as a specific lesson plan for the Character Map. If you're interested in a more complete resource on this topic, refer to my book, *Laura Candler's Graphic Organizers for Reading*, which includes directions for using a variety of specific graphic organizers.

One word of caution—graphic organizers are powerful, but sometimes they are overused in the reading classroom. When included as a part of Reading Workshop, graphic organizers should be introduced slowly, over several days, in order to preserve daily independent reading time. To do this, chunk the lessons into ten- to fifteen-minute blocks to fit them into your daily mini-lesson. After students know how to use a particular graphic organizer, they can use it as their response to reading instead of Book Notes, journals, or other types of response.

Basic Graphic Organizer Introduction

1 WHOLE GROUP – Introduce each new graphic organizer by modeling it with the entire class. Read a book aloud and use input from students to complete each section. Depending on the time allotted for this activity, you may want to have students copy the details onto their own blank graphic organizers to save as a reference for the future. Be sure to save your own example as well.

2 PARTNERS – The next day, pair students and give them one blank copy of the graphic organizer. Display the class example and review the steps for completing it. Read aloud a new text or continue the text from the previous day. This time, have them take turns completing the parts of the organizer together.

3 **INDIVIDUALS** – Finally, provide opportunities for students to use the graphic organizer with the books they are reading during their independent reading time.

Sample Graphic Organizer Lesson

You can introduce the Character Map on page 118 using the story *Jack and the Beanstalk*. I love the version written and illustrated by Steven Kellogg. It's perfect for older elementary and middle school students because the illustrations are scary and gory, and the text includes challenging vocabulary.

1 **PRESENT CHARACTER TRAITS LIST** – Give your students a copy of the Character Traits list on page 117 to use a reference during the lesson.

2 **STUDENTS RECORD CHARACTER TRAITS** – As you read the story aloud to the class, have them jot down character traits for Jack, as well as supporting details, on scrap paper or individual dry-erase boards.

CHARACTER TRAITS

absent-minded	dreamer	mischievous
adventurous	energetic	obedient
anxious	even-tempered	outgoing
ambitious	friendly	outspoken
argumentative	fun-loving	open-minded
bashful	generous	optimistic
bold	gentle	patient
bossy	greedy	patriotic
brave	gullible	persistent
caring	handsome	pessimistic
careless	happy	polite
cautious	hard-working	proud
cheerful	helpful	reckless
clever	heroic	resourceful
clumsy	honest	respectful
conceited	humble	rude
confident	humorous	selfish
considerate	imaginative	serious
content	impatient	shy
courageous	impulsive	sly
cranky	independent	sneaky
creative	innocent	spendthrift
critical	intelligent	spoiled
cruel	inventive	stingy
curious	joyful	stubborn
dainty	lazy	studious
daring	leader	successful
dedicated	logical	suspicious
defiant	lovable	thoughtful
demanding	loving	timid
determined	loyal	unruly
devious	mannerly	unselfish
dishonest	messy	wasteful
disrespectful	methodical	witty

3 **INTRODUCE GRAPHIC ORGANIZER TO CLASS** – Display a blank copy of the Character Map and write "Jack" in the octagon. Ask students to show their dry-erase boards and choose one character trait to use as an example. For example, someone might have written that Jack is brave because he climbed up the beanstalk. Write that information on the chart along with the page number of the supporting detail. Continue calling on students and filling in the chart with character traits and details. (See example on page 119.) Alternatively, you can have students bring their dry-erase boards with them to a small guided reading group where you'll follow the same steps.

4 **COMPLETE CHARACTER MAP IN PAIRS** – The next day, create pairs of students to work together, making sure that any student who generally struggles in reading has a stronger partner or adult helper. Give the pair one Character Map to share between them. Reread or review the story, but this time have them each

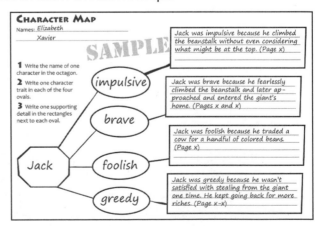

list character traits that describe the ogre. Next, ask them to compare what they wrote with their partner and choose four character traits to use on the Character Map. One person writes "Ogre" in the octagon and then both of them take turns adding the character traits and details to the chart. For example, one person will add the first character trait and detail, then the other person will add the second character trait

and supporting detail. As they take turns, they should be discussing the information that is being added to the graphic organizer. It's helpful if they each write in a different color.

5 **INDIVIDUALS COMPLETE CHARACTER MAPS** – Finally, give each student one blank copy of the Character Map. Have each student complete it independently using a character from a story he or she is currently reading or another read-aloud selection. Allow students to share their work with another student or in a small guided reading group.

Graphic Organizer Examples

Graphic organizers help you organize information. You can create 2-D flat graphic organizers on a sheet of paper, or you can cut and fold paper to create 3-D folded graphic organizers. They often have flaps that can be lifted to display information.

2-D Graphic Organizers

- Venn Diagrams
- Character Maps
- Storyboards
- Story Plot Maps
- T-charts
- Flow Maps
- Multi-Column Charts
- Cause and Effect Maps
- KWL Charts
- Time Lines

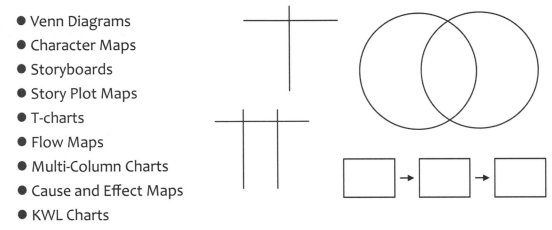

3-D Folded Graphic Organizers

These can often be used to replace the well-known graphic organizers listed above. For example, the two-flap folded graphic organizer can be used instead of the T-chart, and the long folded strip of paper can be used as a time line. Be creative!

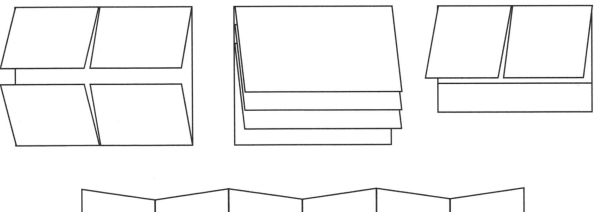

CHARACTER TRAITS

absent-minded	dreamer	mischievous
adventurous	energetic	obedient
anxious	even-tempered	outgoing
ambitious	friendly	outspoken
argumentative	fun-loving	open-minded
bashful	generous	optimistic
bold	gentle	patient
bossy	greedy	patriotic
brave	gullible	persistent
caring	handsome	pessimistic
careless	happy	polite
cautious	hard-working	proud
cheerful	helpful	reckless
clever	heroic	resourceful
clumsy	honest	respectful
conceited	humble	rude
confident	humorous	selfish
considerate	imaginative	serious
content	impatient	shy
courageous	impulsive	sly
cranky	independent	sneaky
creative	innocent	spendthrift
critical	intelligent	spoiled
cruel	inventive	stingy
curious	joyful	stubborn
dainty	lazy	studious
daring	leader	successful
dedicated	logical	suspicious
defiant	lovable	thoughtful
demanding	loving	timid
determined	loyal	unruly
devious	mannerly	unselfish
dishonest	messy	wasteful
disrespectful	methodical	witty

CHARACTER MAP

Names: _____

1 Write the name of one character in the octagon.

2 Write one character trait in each of the four ovals.

3 Write one supporting detail in the rectangles next to each oval.

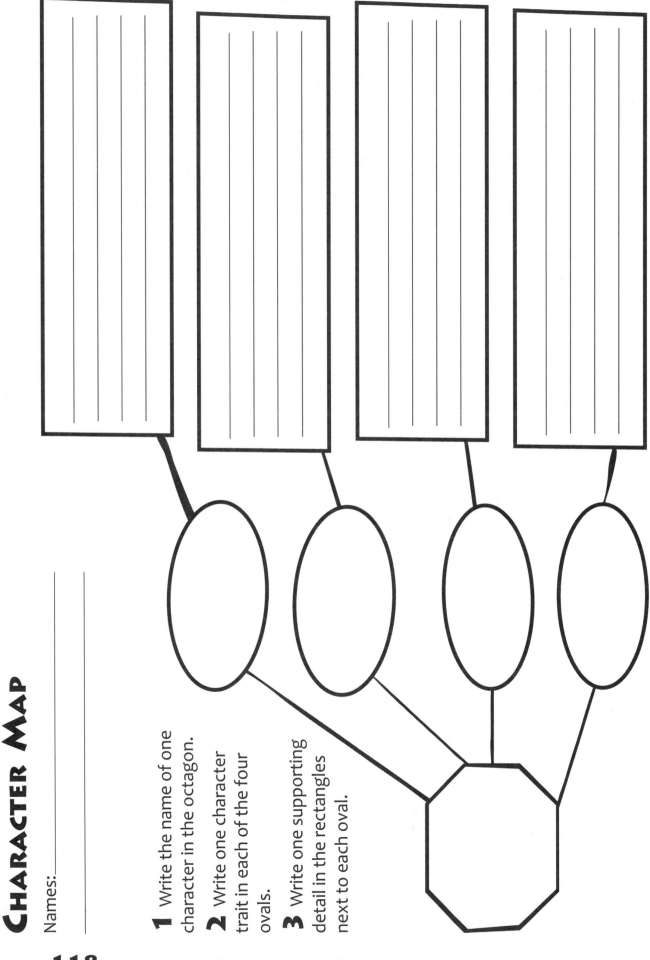

Character Map

Names: _Elizabeth_
Xavier

SAMPLE

1 Write the name of one character in the octagon.

2 Write one character trait in each of the four ovals.

3 Write one supporting detail in the rectangles next to each oval.

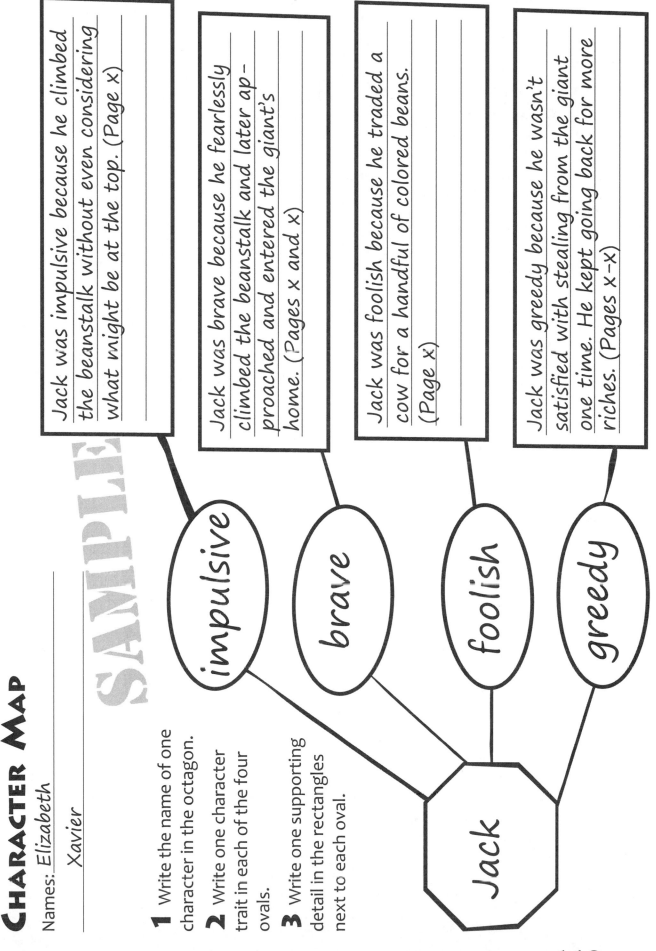

Jack was impulsive because he climbed the beanstalk without even considering what might be at the top. (Page x)

Jack was brave because he fearlessly climbed the beanstalk and later approached and entered the giant's home. (Pages x and x)

Jack was foolish because he traded a cow for a handful of colored beans. (Page x)

Jack was greedy because he wasn't satisfied with stealing from the giant one time. He kept going back for more riches. (Pages x-x)

impulsive

brave

foolish

greedy

Jack

POWER READING TOOL 11 Self Assessment

Self Assessment is one of the most powerful tools to motivate and encourage students. It is not designed to replace objective, skill-based tests; rather, it is a way to encourage students to take responsibility for their own learning.

Self-assessment tools should be introduced only after you've been using the Reading Workshop model regularly for at least a month. Younger children may not be ready for this step for many months, and you would have to adapt the assessment forms to make them simpler.

There are two different self-assessment forms as part of this Power Reading Tool. Choose the form that works best for your students. Page 121 is a Reading Self Assessment in which the student rates his/her progress with Reading Workshop on a scale from 1 to 5. Page 122 shows a Reading Workshop Evaluation with maximum total points of 100. Page 123 shows a more customizable version of this same form. You can reproduce these pages or download these forms from my website (www.lauracandler.com/prw).

Materials

- Reading Workshop Evaluations or Reading Self Assessments

- Power Reading Logs

What to Do:

1 When you feel the time is right, choose the evaluation form that best meets your needs. Distribute the form and ask students to open their Power Reading Logs.

2 Ask your students to examine their Book Challenge charts and My Weekly Reading Goals forms for evidence of reading progress. Have they met their goals? Are they making progress?

3 Talk them through every section of the assessment form, explaining how to complete each part and where to look in the Power Reading Log for evidence of progress. Be very specific about what you want them to write in each section. You might even display a copy of the form and model the kinds of things to write, but beware of writing so much that your students just copy your model.

4 Collect the forms and use them as the basis for individual conferences. Whether or not you assign a grade to the self assessment is a decision for you to make. I see nothing wrong with grading this assessment, as long as each student understands what he or she needs to do to improve. Self assessment is instrumental for celebrating successes, as well as encouraging students to refocus their efforts to improve.

Reading Self Assessment

Name _____ Date _____

Rate yourself from 1 to 5 in each of the following areas of the Power Reading Workshop.

	Low				High
Listening to read alouds and participating in mini-lessons	1	2	3	4	5
Being prepared with book when RW begins	1	2	3	4	5
Staying focused and reading for the entire SSR time	1	2	3	4	5
Use of reading strategies to understand the text	1	2	3	4	5
Length and/or difficulty of reading selections	1	2	3	4	5
Variety of genres including fiction and nonfiction	1	2	3	4	5
Quality and quantity of written responses	1	2	3	4	5
Evidence of accurate and timely record-keeping	1	2	3	4	5

Write a paragraph analyzing your recent progress as a reader. Be sure to give specific examples to support your analysis. Include the books you've been reading and the strategies you've been using since your last assessment.

_____

_____

_____

_____

_____

_____

_____

_____

_____

Teacher Comments

_____

_____

_____

_____

READING WORKSHOP EVALUATION

Name _____ Date _____

Criteria	Max Points	My Points
Reading Workshop Participation (Choosing a book before Reading Workshop, staying in one spot, staying on task, completing Book Notes, not bothering others) I think I deserve_____ points because_____ _____ _____ _____	60	
Book Selection (Book difficulty, total number of pages read, grade level appropriateness, variety of genres, fiction and nonfiction, etc.) I think I deserve_____ points because_____ _____ _____ _____	20	
Written Response and Record-Keeping (Filling out Reading Log accurately, quality of written response, completing Book Notes, etc.) I think I deserve_____ points because_____ _____ _____ _____	20	
	100	

Teacher Comments_____
_____
_____

READING WORKSHOP EVALUATION

Name _____ Date _____

Criteria	Max Points	My Points
I think I deserve_____ points because_____ _____ _____ _____		
I think I deserve_____ points because_____ _____ _____ _____		
I think I deserve_____ points because_____ _____ _____ _____		

Teacher Comments _____

_____

_____

POWER READING TOOL 12 · Strategic Planning

The key to an effective Reading Workshop is planning. The first several months of your workshop will be organized around the basic introduction to Reading Workshop and the Power Reading Tools, but then what? Observe your students as you interact with them, and you'll discover exactly what they need in the way of skill or strategy instruction. For example, if your students are reluctant to read nonfiction books, perhaps they need additional work recognizing and using nonfiction text features. If they take weeks to finish a single book, perhaps they need additional support for choosing appropriate books that interest them. Take notes as you interact with your students during small group instruction and conferences, and you'll have more mini-lesson ideas than you have time to teach!

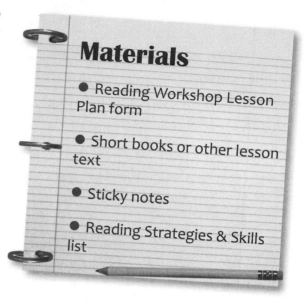

Materials

● Reading Workshop Lesson Plan form

● Short books or other lesson text

● Sticky notes

● Reading Strategies & Skills list

What to Do:

Take time to plan your mini-lessons in advance, so you focus on your objectives for each lesson. The form on page 127 will help you organize your plans.

1 Use the list of suggested skills and strategies on page 126 to help you select a focus for your lesson.

2 Identify a short text that offers an opportunity to teach that particular objective. (See sample plan on page 128.)

3 Teach the mini-lesson using the vocabulary, concepts, or information found in that text.

READING WORKSHOP LESSON PLAN

Date _____   Mon Tues Wed Thurs Fri

Objective _____

Skill or Strategy Focus _____

Book and/or Materials Needed _____

Mini-Lesson Description _____
_____
_____
_____

Independent Reading Focus and Response _____
_____
_____

Individual Conference Plans (Who and What) _____
_____
_____
_____

Other Notes _____
_____
_____

4 Follow up by challenging students to use the skill or strategy as they read their own books that day. Ask them to record evidence of their learning on a sticky note, in a journal, or on their Book Notes form.

5 Discuss the focus skill with your students when you meet with them individually or in small groups.

Sample Lesson Plan

The character trait mini-lesson described in Power Reading Tool 10, Graphic Organizers, can be further developed to follow this general format. First, teach the character trait lesson using *Jack and the Beanstalk* and the Character Map graphic organizer. After the mini-lesson, challenge students to think about the characters in their own books. Tell them that after they finish reading for the day, you want them to mark two passages that show a particular character trait. They should place the sticky notes in the book where they found the supporting details. Use these as a focus for your next conference with them. Page 128 shows this lesson as you might write it on the Reading Workshop Lesson Plan.

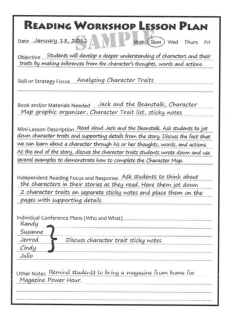

Writing Your Own Lesson Plans

Create your own mini-lessons by following this basic structure and adapting it to your needs. Use the form on page 127 as an outline of the basic lesson components. If you need ideas for mini-lessons, there are numerous resources available to you in print and on the web. *Revisiting the Reading Workshop* by Barbara Orehovec and Marybeth Alley is an excellent resource with loads of mini-lessons. *Reading Power* by Adrienne Gear is another wonderful resource.

> **As you use Reading Workshop concepts and Power Reading Tools with your students, you'll undoubtedly develop your own power tools to motivate and challenge your class. If you create a new twist on Reading Workshop, please email me at laura@lauracandler.com and let me know what's working for you. Until then, keep sharing the joy of reading!**

Reading Strategies & Skills

❑ Summarizing

❑ Making predictions

❑ Making inferences

❑ Sequencing events

❑ Determining cause and effect

❑ Finding the problem and solution

❑ Distinguishing between fact and opinion

❑ Recognizing elements of fiction (plot, setting, characters, theme, mood)

❑ Recognizing various genres (folklore, autobiographies, mysteries, biographies, fantasies, historical fiction, science fiction, fables, etc.)

❑ Using context clues to infer word meanings

❑ Recognizing figurative language (similes, metaphors, personification, etc.)

❑ Analyzing character goals and traits

❑ Finding topic, main idea, and supporting details

❑ Determining the author's purpose

❑ Recognizing propaganda

Reading Workshop Lesson Plan

Date _____   Mon   Tues   Wed   Thurs   Fri

Objective _____

_____

Skill or Strategy Focus_____

_____

Book and/or Materials Needed _____

_____

Mini-lesson Description _____

_____

_____

_____

_____

Independent Reading Focus and Response_____

_____

_____

_____

Individual Conference Plans (Who and What)_____

_____

_____

_____

_____

_____

Other Notes _____

_____

_____

_____

READING WORKSHOP LESSON PLAN

Date _January 18, 2011_   Mon (Tues) Wed Thurs Fri

Objective _Students will develop a deeper understanding of characters and their traits by making inferences from the character's thoughts, words, and actions._

Skill or Strategy Focus _Analyzing Character Traits_

Book and/or Materials Needed _Jack and the Beanstalk, Character Map graphic organizer, Character Traits list, sticky notes_

Mini-lesson Description _Read aloud Jack and the Beanstalk. Ask students to jot down character traits and supporting details from the story. Discuss the fact that we can learn about a character through his or her thoughts, words, and actions. At the end of the story, discuss the character traits students wrote down and use several examples to demonstrate how to complete the Character Map._

Independent Reading Focus and Response_Ask students to think about the characters in their stories as they read. Have them jot down 2 character traits on separate sticky notes and place them on the pages with supporting details._

Individual Conference Plans (Who and What)_____
Randy
Suzanne
Jerrod   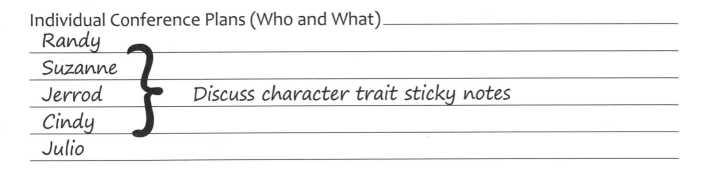 Discuss character trait sticky notes
Cindy
Julio

Other Notes _Remind students to bring a magazine from home for Magazine Power Hour._

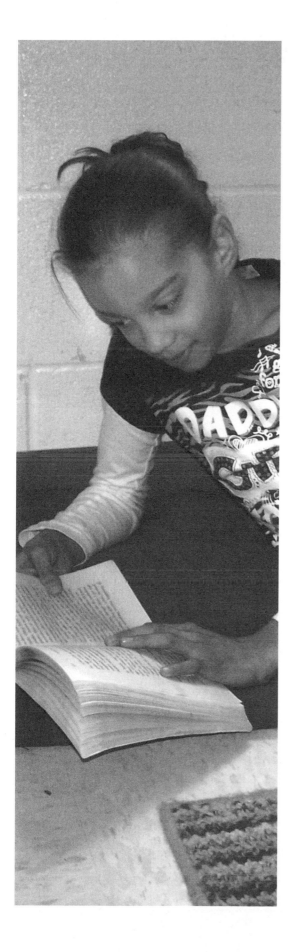

Additional Resources

Name _____ Date _____

ACTIVITIES AND INTERESTS

Read each activity description. Place a check in the column to show how much you enjoy this activity or how closely it describes you. (1 is the lowest score and 5 is the highest score.) If you have never done the activity, make a guess or place a check in the *Not Sure* column.

Activity Description	1	2	3	4	5	Not Sure
Reading adventure stories						
Building models						
Playing outside						
Putting together puzzles						
Reading about weather or weather systems						
Reading about animals						
Reading short chapter books						
Watching television						
Reading "how to" books						
Writing stories						
Reading about disgusting or gross topics						
Reading mysteries or detective stories						
Riding a bicycle						
Reading magazines						
Reading about drawing or crafts						
Reading comic books						
Reading about far away places						
Reading about plants						
Playing with animals						
Reading about friends and friendship						
Playing word games or doing word puzzles						
Solving math problems						
Writing poetry						

More Activity Descriptions	1	2	3	4	5	Not Sure
Reading fantasy books or stories						
Taking pictures or recording video						
Reading about fashion						
Playing a musical instrument						
Going shopping						
Reading about famous people						
Reading science fiction (aliens, space, etc.)						
Drawing or painting						
Reading about science topics (nonfiction)						
Listening to music						
Playing video games						
Cooking or preparing food						
Reading about sports						
Playing sports						
Going to museums						
Reading funny books						
Going to the movies						
Reading about real places						
Reading about cars or motorcycles						
Reading about the military or war						
Reading long chapter books						
Going camping						
Using the Internet						
Talking or texting on the phone						
Going to the public library						
Going swimming						
Spending time with friends						
Doing things to earn extra money						

Certificate of Award

Congratulations to

_____

for meeting your

40-BOOK CHALLENGE GOAL

Celebrate the joy of reading!

_____
Teacher

_____
Date

Certificate of Award

Congratulations to

_____

for meeting your
20-Book Challenge Goal
Celebrate the joy of reading!

_____ Date

_____ Teacher

Certificate of Award

Congratulations to

_____

for meeting your
BOOK CHALLENGE GOAL
Celebrate the joy of reading!

_____
Teacher

_____
Date

PROFESSIONAL READING

These books are excellent resources for your professional collection. Many of them provide detailed explanations of different aspects of the Reading Workshop approach as well as effective classroom management. The methods in *Laura Candler's Power Reading Workshop* will allow you to launch a workshop quickly, but you'll want to develop a deeper understanding of this model by reading some of these great books.

Candler, Laura. *Laura Candler's Graphic Organizers for Reading.* St. Johnsbury, VT: Compass, 2012.

Fountas, Irene C., and Gay Su Pinnell. *Guiding Readers and Writers: Teaching Comprehension, Genre, and Content Literacy.* Portsmouth, NH: Heinemann, 2001.

Gallagher, Kelly. *Readicide: How Schools Are Killing Reading and What You Can Do About It.* Portland, ME: Stenhouse, 2009.

Gear, Adrienne. *Nonfiction Reading Power: Teaching Students How to Think While They Read All Kinds of Information.* Markham, ON: Pembroke, 2008.

Gear, Adrienne. *Reading Power: Teaching Students to Think While They Read.* Markham, ON: Pembroke, 2006.

Harvey, Stephanie, and Anne Goudvis. *Strategies That Work: Teaching Comprehension for Understanding and Engagement.* Portland, ME: Stenhouse, 2007.

Jones, Fredric H., Patrick Jones, and Jo Lynne Talbott Jones. *Tools for Teaching: Discipline, Instruction, Motivation.* Santa Cruz, CA: F.H. Jones & Associates, 2007.

Kagan, Spencer. *Cooperative Learning.* San Juan Capistrano, CA: Kagan Cooperative Learning, 1994.

Layne, Steven L. *Igniting a Passion for Reading: Successful Strategies for Building Lifetime Readers.* Portland, ME: Stenhouse, 2009.

Miller, Donalyn. *The Book Whisperer: Awakening the Inner Reader in Every Child.* San Francisco, CA: Jossey-Bass, 2009.

Orehovec, Barbara, and Marybeth Alley. *Revisiting the Reading Workshop: Management, Mini-Lessons, and Strategies.* New York: Scholastic, 2003.

Schulman, Mary Browning. *Guided Reading in Grades 3-6: Everything You Need to Make Small-Group Reading Instruction Work in Your Classroom.* New York: Teaching Resources, 2006.

Wong, Harry K., Rosemary T. Wong, and Chelonnda Seroyer. *The First Days of School: How to Be an Effective Teacher.* Mountain View, CA: Harry K. Wong Publications, 2009.

INTERNET RESOURCES

"Beth Newingham's Third Grade." Beth Newingham, Hill Elementary School, Troy, Michigan
http://hill.troy.k12.mi.us/staff/bnewingham/myweb3
Great teacher blog with links to resources for Reading Workshop and other literacy lessons.

"Education World ® News for YOU." Education World
http://www.educationworld.com/a_lesson/archives/newsforyou.shtml
Excellent source for short informational feature articles that appeal to students. The articles aren't very current, but they are great for mini-lessons or guided reading.

"ReadWriteThink."
http://www.readwritethink.org
This website contains lesson plans and resources for reading and writing lessons and activities. It provides professional development and parent/home resources.

"BBC CBeebies – Jack and the Beanstalk."
http://www.bbc.co.uk/cbeebies/misc/stories/jackandthebeanstalk
This is a short animated version of Jack and the Beanstalk, *perfect for mini-lessons.*

"Readers and Writers Workshop." Jennifer Myers
http://quest.carnegiefoundation.org/~dpointer/jennifermyers/workshopapproach.htm
There are videos on this site to correlate with each aspect of Reading Workshop.

"Teaching Tools." The Reading Lady
http://www.readinglady.com/mosaic/tools/tools.htm
An outstanding collection of helpful tools and resources for reading instruction. Rubrics, lesson plans, assessment tools, and more.

"Nancy Fetzer's Literacy Connections." Nancy Fetzer
http://www.nancyfetzer.com
This website is interactive with videos, downloadables, and blogs about literacy issues, writer's workshop, and reading connections.

"Reading Workshop Strategies." Teaching Resources
http://www.lauracandler.com/strategies/readingworkshop.php
Includes an overview of the Reading Workshop approach as well as a variety of printables and other helpful resources.

"Schoolwide Enrichment Model-Reading." Center for Gifted Education and Talent Development, University of Connecticut
http://www.gifted.uconn.edu/SEMR/using bookmarks.html
Excellent collection of bookmarks that can be used to encourage analytical thinking and discussion.

"Storyline Online."
http://www.storylineonline.net
On this interactive website, two dozen popular picture books are read aloud by famous people. You'll find Thank You, Mr. Falker, Enemy Pie, Stellaluna, *and more.*

BOOKS FOR THE FIRST TEN DAYS

DAY 1

Polacco, Patricia. *Thank You, Mr. Falker*. New York: Philomel, 2001.
> *This autobiographical story is about a child with dyslexia who finds her love for reading because of a supportive teacher.*

Thaler, Mike, and Jared D. Lee. *The Teacher from the Black Lagoon*. New York: Scholastic, 2008.
> *A student is fearful of his first day of school only to arrive and find his teacher is not a hideous monster.*

DAY 2

Cannon, Janell. *Crickwing*. Boston, MA: Houghton Mifflin Harcourt, 2010.
> *A cockroach with a crooked wing is mean to other insects and gets himself taken prisoner. It's a powerful book that deals with bullying.*

Pfister, Marcus. *The Rainbow Fish*. New York: North-South, 1992.
> *A selfish fish will not share his shiny scales. Ultimately, the rainbow fish learns how to be a friend to others.*

DAY 3

Hopkins, Jackie, and John Manders. *Goldie Socks and the Three Libearians*. Fort Atkinson, WI: Upstart, 2007.
> *The picture book story of a little girl who enters the home of a book-loving family of bear librarians.*

Miller, Pat, and Nadine Bernard Westcott. *We're Going on a Book Hunt*. Fort Atkinson, WI: Upstart, 2008.
> *This picture book for young children introduces library procedures to students not familiar with a school library.*

DAY 4

Henkes, Kevin. *Chrysanthemum*. New York: Greenwillow, 2007.
> *Chrysanthemum is a kindergartener who gets picked on because of her name and finds support in her family.*

McCloud, Carol, and David Messing. *Have You Filled a Bucket Today? A Guide to Daily Happiness for Kids*. Northville, MI: Ferne, 2009.
> *This heartwarming book encourages positive behavior as children see how rewarding it is to express daily kindness, appreciation, and love.*

DAY 5

Bunting, Eve, and Ronald Himler. *Train to Somewhere*. New York: Clarion, 1996.
> *A story about the journey of orphans that travel by train from the east coast to the west to their adoptive families.*

Van Allsburg, Chris. *The Wretched Stone*. Boston: Houghton Mifflin, 1991.
> *A story written in the form of captain's logs about a glowing stone and its effects on his ship's sailors. Students can make connections to how people behave with TV and other "toys" that consume their attention.*

DAY 6

Cronin, Doreen, and Harry Bliss. *Diary of a Worm*. New York, NY: Joanna Cotler, 2003.
   Life from a worm's point of view.

Munson, Derek, and Tara Calahan King. *Enemy Pie*. San Francisco: Chronicle, 2000.
   A boy discovers, with his dad's help, that the best way to get rid of an enemy is to make him a friend.

DAY 7

Scieszka, Jon, and Lane Smith. *The True Story of the Three Little Pigs*. New York: Puffin, 1996.
   A twist on the traditional tale, told from the point of view of the wolf.

Wiesner, David. *Tuesday*. New York: Clarion, 1991.
   This book is about a group of frogs flying through the air one night.

DAY 8

Cannon, Janell. *Stellaluna*. Boston: Houghton Mifflin Harcourt, 2010.
   Wonderful story of a baby bat who falls into a bird's nest. She tries to be like the baby birds in the nest but things don't work out. Great for comparing and contrasting bats and birds.

Gibbons, Gail. *Bats*. New York: Holiday House, 1999.
   Nonfiction book about bats. Great for using after reading Stellaluna *to discuss the difference between fiction and nonfiction.*

DAY 9

Fletcher, Ralph J., and April Ward. *A Writing Kind of Day: Poems for Young Poets*. Honesdale, PA: Wordsong/Boyds Mills, 2005.
   Excellent collection of poems that will appeal to students in fourth grade and above. Poems are about real life situations and provide lots of opportunities for connections.

Prelutsky, Jack, and Arnold Lobel. *The Random House Book of Poetry for Children*. New York: Random House Children's, 2000.
   Excellent collection of poetry for children of all ages. Includes examples with imagery, rhyme, metaphors, similes, and personification, as well as funny poems.

DAY 10

Krull, Kathleen, and David Diaz. *Wilma Unlimited: How Wilma Rudolph Became the World's Fastest Woman*. San Diego: Harcourt Brace, 1996.
   Inspiring biography on Wilma Rudolph, one of the world's fastest women. Wilma overcame polio and went on to win gold in the Olympics.

Wulffson, Don L. *The Kid Who Invented the Popsicle: And Other Surprising Stories about Inventions*. New York: Cobblehill /Dutton, 1997.
   Nonfiction book about the amazing stories behind some common inventions.

Books For Older Readers

This list includes picture books that may appeal to upper elementary or middle school students. These titles were suggested by the members of the Empowering Readers Learning Community to assist teachers of older students in finding short selections suitable for mini-lessons.

Bunting, Eve, and Donald Carrick. *The Wednesday Surprise*. New York: Clarion, 1989.
> *A girl teaches her elderly grandmother how to read.*

Bunting, Eve, and Ronald Himler. *Fly Away Home*. New York: Clarion, 1991.
> *This book takes a look at homelessness through the eyes of a homeless boy and his father who live at an airport. It's a touching but difficult book that is not recommended for younger students.*

Bunting, Eve, and Ronald Himler. *Train to Somewhere*. New York: Clarion, 1996.
> *Story of a group of orphans on the Orphan Train in the old West.*

Bunting, Eve, and Beth Peck. *How Many Days to America? A Thanksgiving Story*. New York: Clarion, 1988.
> *A refugee family is crossing the ocean on a small boat, trying to make it to America.*

Bunting, Eve, and Irving Toddy. *Cheyenne Again*. New York: Clarion, 1995.
> *This book is about how early Americans sent Native Americans to boarding school because the children were "too Indian."*

Fox, Mem, and Julie Vivas. *Wilfrid Gordon McDonald Partridge*. Brooklyn, NY: Kane/Miller, 1989.
> *A boy who lives next to a retirement home helps a woman remember items from her past.*

Gerstein, Mordicai. *The Man Who Walked between the Towers*. New York: Square Fish, 2007.
> *The amazing true story of Philippe Petit's tightrope walk between Manhattan's World Trade Center towers in 1974.*

Hopkinson, Deborah. *Sweet Clara and the Freedom Quilt*. New York: Alfred A. Knopf, 1995.
> *Follows the story of a young slave girl, Clara, who works as a seamstress on a southern plantation. She pieces together clues about her surroundings and stitches a quilt that serves as a map to freedom.*

Kellogg, Steven. *Jack and the Beanstalk*. New York: Morrow Junior, 1991.
> *This particular version of Jack and the Beanstalk will appeal to older students due to Steven Kellogg's artistic style. The ogre and his wife are horrifying in their appearance and the poem chanted by the ogre has all the gory details of the original folk tale.*

Martin, Rafe, and David Shannon. *The Rough-Face Girl*. New York: G.P. Putnam's Sons, 1992.
> *This is the Algonquin Indian version of the Cinderella story, in which two cruel sisters mistreat their younger sister, the Rough-Face Girl. She is named this because the sparks from tending the fire have scarred her skin. This story is excellent for discussions regarding the importance of valuing people for what's inside them rather than for their appearance.*

McCann, Michelle Roehm, and Ann E. Marshall. *Luba: The Angel of Bergen-Belsen*. Berkeley, CA: Tricycle, 2003.
> *This book is about a woman during the Holocaust and an account of being a prisoner. She finds fifty-four babies left in a field to die and is able to save fifty-two of them until the camp was liberated by the British.*

Polacco, Patricia. *Junkyard Wonders*. New York: Philomel, 2010.
> *In this story, Trisha moves to a new school and discovers that her new classroom is called "the junkyard." However, her amazing teacher makes each student feel treasured and unique.*

Polacco, Patricia. *Pink and Say*. New York: Scholastic, 1994.
> *This book is a touching historical fiction story that takes place during the Civil War. Sheldon, a fifteen-year-old white boy is rescued from the battlefield by Pinkus, a young African-American soldier, and the two become friends.*

Turner, Ann Warren, and Ronald Himler. *Nettie's Trip South*. New York: Macmillan, 1987.
> *A girl from the North visits relatives in the South and is appalled at seeing slavery firsthand.*

Wisniewski, David. *Secret Knowledge of Grownups*. New York: Harper Collins, 1998.
> *This hilarious story explains the "true" meaning behind the rules that grown-ups tell kids, such as "Eat your vegetables," and "Don't play with your food."*

Wyeth, Sharon Dennis, and Chris K. Soentpiet. *Something Beautiful*. New York: Dragonfly, 2002.
> *In this touching story, an inner-city girl finds her neighborhood ugly and decides to go looking for something beautiful. She polls the neighbors who share with her many beautiful aspects of their lives.*

Yin, and Chris K. Soentpiet. *Coolies*. New York: Puffin, 2003.
> *It tells about the building of the Trans-American railroad and the great effort put forth by the Chinese immigrants. It also lets you know how people in America were very prejudiced against the Chinese immigrants.*

Yolen, Jane, Heidi E. Y. Stemple, and Roger Roth. *The Mary Celeste: An Unsolved Mystery from History*. New York: Simon & Schuster for Young Readers, 2002.
> *This is an historical fiction story in picture book form that's based on fact. It explores the unsolved mystery surrounding the disappearance of the crew of the Mary Celeste in 1872.*